More
Than A
Dream

More Than A Dream

Paul Greenhalgh

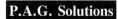
P.A.G. Solutions

First published 2005 by
PAG Solutions Ltd
75 Bolton Street
Ramsbottom
Bury
Lancashire BL0 9HY

ISBN 0 9550 9170 5

Design, typesetting and production by
Action Publishing Technology Ltd, Gloucester

Printed and bound in Great Britain

Contents

Acknowledgements

Thanks firstly to Graham Briggs and Tom Barras and their respective families. Without their support and enduring patience the book would quite simply not have been possible. I wish you all success and happiness in the future.

Similarly, I am indebted to the Dave Rayner Fund, in particular Dudley Hayton and Keith Lambert. Their endorsement of the project gave it some much needed credibility and helped ease my way into the cycling fraternity. The Fund does a worthy job and many a rider is in its debt, as now am I.

My friend Toni Mion, Hamish Haynes, Roger Hammond, Jez Hunt, the GB under 23 squad, assorted Aussie cyclists and Dan Fleeman all played their part and I thank them too.

I can't, of course, forget Cheeky Phil Evans. His adventures set off my own inquisitiveness and laid the foundations for the book. I look forward to our next meeting, whether it is in Manchester or la Manche.

Thanks most of all go to Julia. It was an honour to have you with me on this life-affirming trip. Here's to many more, my love!

Dedication

This book is dedicated to the late Dave Rayner.

CHAPTER 1

Phil Evans and Me

JUNE 2002. A CLOUDY Sunday morning at Rivington, just outside Bolton. My partner, Julia, and I are part of a sparse crowd there to watch the British Cycling Elite Road Race Championships. It is late morning and the race is still in its early stages. Taking in the scene near the finishing line, one can tell in an instant that cycling is a minority sport in Britain. The crowd can be counted in the tens or perhaps low hundreds and the large array of crash barriers that surround the course seem something on an over-reaction to the numbers actually here. There are only one or two food outlets in place too, serving up snacks to the small but ever-hungry groups of cyclists that have ridden over to the race from their usual Sunday morning meeting points. The official race programme also tells its own tale. It is a simple affair printed on paper, rather than the glossy product that you might expect to find at an event of this importance. The contents amount to a list of the riders, a map of the course and not much more. The information is interspersed with one or two advertisements for the mostly local companies and cycling bodies that have helped with the sponsorship and organisation of the event.

The race is still to take shape and consequently the field is still in one large group. Wave upon wave of racing cyclists cruise across the Start–Finish line, cutting through the grey in a mass of colour and gleaming metal. The riders are slim. This is the highlight of the year for many and you can tell that they have trained hard for the race. They carry no excess weight and sit easily upon their elegant and expensive racing bikes. Like swans their upper bodies are still, whilst their legs thrash about in a whirl of movement.

We are there to watch David Millar. He is one of the few British riders who has made it as a professional in Europe and he rides in France for the Cofidis team. Millar has won big races, including stages of the Grand Tours of Spain and France and he rarely competes in Britain. There are simply too few races that are big enough to tempt him and his team over the channel. He is here today though with one team-mate (another Briton named Rob Hayles), taking the opportunity to get to know the course, as it is to be used later in the summer when Manchester hosts the Commonwealth Games. In the end he will not ride in the Games, due to the accumulated effects of three weeks of racing in the Tour de France, but at this point he is a live prospect for the gold medal in the road race and also his speciality, the individual time trial.

The field disappears down the hill and into the distance as another lap begins. Save for one or two early stragglers, who will not survive to see the later stages of the race, the group is in one piece. The race is over one hundred miles in length and the majority of the competitors are still riding within themselves at this point, but to the uninitiated such as us the pace is high. We haven't seen Millar yet and we know that he would be instantly recognisable. Taller than many of his adversaries and wearing the red, white and blue colours of his team, he cuts the figure of a tanned European cycling King among a field of domestic Princes. After some minutes he appears in the distance somewhere up the tree-lined road. He's not going at any pace. It is clear that even at this stage his race is over. He climbs off. It was a bad day, we later learn. What do we do now?

Our eyes return to the race programme and we look through the list of riders. There are one or two familiar names but these are mostly men that compete only on the domestic scene. Big fish in the small pond of British cycling. To put it simply, with Millar already heading for the showers, there are only a few people in the race that you have seen on the TV or read about in the national press. This though, says more about the stature of cycling in the UK than about the riders themselves. We run through the list looking for someone else to support and after some seconds our eyes fall on the name of Philip Evans. Actually it's not the name so much as the club he represents which captures our attention. Philip Evans rides for UC Briquebec in France. Unlike the majority of the field who ride for minor British trade teams or for their local clubs, this rider appears to be representing a French amateur club. We wonder aloud about how he ended up in this position. What is his story? We wonder. How did he end up in France? And at that precise moment in time the flame of curiosity begins to burn. As we stand there in our waterproof coats in the Lancastrian gloom, waiting for the rain to arrive, a trail of serendipitous events is being prepared for us that will, in a small way at least, change lives.

Briquebec, to be precise, is in Basse Normandy. It is about 20 miles due south of Cherbourg on the Cotentin peninsula. Go due west from Briquebec and you will soon reach the coast. Then after a short but choppy sea crossing you would near the island of Jersey. For the past two years we have holidayed in this part of the world after discovering it almost by accident. We have become regular visitors to the weekly street markets and the unassuming shops and bars of this small town and the others in the region of the Manche. And it was in this part of the world that we fell in love with the sea. This is a place where the light can change in an instant from charcoal to a searing white and where the long beaches are unveiled each morning like a bed that has been freshly made just for you. It is far from being the most fashionable part of France, but it is rich in many ways. I remember back to the previous August and riding my bike through the green and fecund lanes of the area. I recall the time that I had to stop in Briquebec for an emergency Pain au Raisin after running out of energy and experiencing a hunger flat (or 'bonk' as it is sometimes known) while out on a long ride. So despite having no idea of who he is, where he is from and how he came to end up riding for UC Briquebec, Philip Evans becomes our man.

The next time the group comes through we look out for him. We don't know what he looks like and anyway the riders are wearing helmets and sunglasses which rob them of their individuality. We are looking, therefore, for a clue in other aspects of his appearance. We don't have long though, as the field is travelling faster this time and it will soon be off down the hill again. And then we spot him. He is towards the back of the bunch in a red and green shirt with Briquebec's most famous landmark, a grand old castle, emblazoned upon it. We have walked around this medieval building that is now a hotel and restaurant on numerous occasions before settling down for a coffee or a glass of locally made cider in one of the bars on the town's cobbled main street.

'Allez Philip Evans!' we shout as he flashes past us. 'Allez!'

We repeat our encouragement when the field comes through once or twice more. However we have other commitments later in the day and have to leave before the end of the race. We make our way back to the car unsure how Philip Evans will fare, but dreaming of a victory for the unknown rider from Briquebec.

Philip Evans did not win that day (Julian Winn from Wales was crowned the Champion), but he stayed in my thoughts over the following weeks. How would a British rider end up in France riding for an amateur club? Why would they go there? How would they find a club? Where would they live and how would they make ends meet? These questions stayed with me over the following months and I couldn't quite shake the need to know more. However, it took the legacy of illness and a series of strange coincidences for my curiosity to coalesce into something coherent.

I am a keen if average cyclist, but at the time of the Rivington race, I had not been able to ride my bike for around five months. After working hard to get fit over the previous winter, at the grand old age of thirty-five I was going to join a cycling club. I was even planning to try my hand at racing. Not to any great standard, of course, but something by which I could experience the buzz of being a competitive bike rider. A few local time trials at which I could live out my dream in the same way that the riders in this race were living out theirs.

This though was now a fading aspiration. A debilitating and undiagnosed complaint had laid me low. From mid-February, fatigue and headaches left me unable to function properly and exercise was simply out of the question. This together with an increased craving for sugary foods meant that in addition to being unwell I was also fat and unhappy. These were dark times and although I could get through the working day (just) it was downhill after that. I was bored with talking to doctors who could tell me what it was not, but not what it was. They were at least able to rule out anything serious, but for a number of months every day was something of a minor ordeal. I'd wake up feeling fine. I'm cured, I would think. Today it will all be over. I'd jump into the car and drive to work believing that it would soon be behind me. That I would be back running and cycling in no time at all on the hilly roads of Ramsbottom where we live. But for ages it just didn't happen. Gradually, as the morning wore on, the headache would return and then I would start to feel tired. Not just faintly drowsy, but fatigued to the extent that pulling myself out of my office chair required an extreme effort. A bar of chocolate would bring me some much called-for energy and I'd continue until the pattern repeated itself in the afternoon. More chocolate would get me through to the end of the day and I would then come home to collapse onto the sofa before heading off to bed at some ridiculously early hour.

To this day I still don't know what was wrong with me. After doing my own research I finally narrowed it down to either the prolonged after effects of a virus (ME to the tabloid press), or a spectacular outbreak of tree pollen allergies, or maybe even a combination of the two. By June and the time of the race though, I was just grateful that the effects were beginning to diminish. The headaches were less intense and the periods of fatigue were shorter and less energy-sapping. I had even sneaked out one evening and tried to run around the local park. I had concocted some story about going for milk, or something, and had then attempted to plod the mile loop between home and there. Over the past few years I had become fairly fit and would look scornfully at the rotund people that one would see jogging at a stupidly slow pace in the park, but now as I was dismayed to find out, I had joined their tribe.

The road back to fitness and to contentment was a long one and my outlook was consciously changed by the unhappy experience I had gone through. To those around me it must have seemed like the life had been sucked out of me and I felt trapped and deprived of the things that I loved doing the most, such as riding the bike. It was also difficult not being able to cope. Friends and loved ones that had previously relied on me, watched as I struggled to offer them the support that they grown to expect. In fact more often than not, it was me that was looking for help and assistance.

I would never say that what happened to me was a good thing. How can you say that about illness? However, I also know that had I not lived through those bleak months in 2002, I would not have taken the risks required to write this book. I would not have acted on my natural inquisitiveness and gone on to find out more about Philip Evans and would not in turn have been so richly rewarded for being nosey. In this respect, I have to offer a grudging thank you to whatever it was that turned my world upside down. Being ill brought me, albeit via a circuitous route, to the people and events that make up this tale and at the same time my recovery has been characterised by a kind of zeal derived from the desire to make up for lost time.

By July 2002 I was almost totally recovered, save for the odd headache and the gained weight. I was riding my bike over short distances and was working my way back into the routines that had been off-limits to me earlier in the year. As part of this I had arranged to spend the final weekend of the Tour de France in Paris with my brother. Malcolm and I would watch the peloton stream down the Champs Elysées and be part of the mass of people there to celebrate a sport and a way of life that they love. The experience was all that we hoped it would be and spurred on by a wonderful weekend of sun, cycling and beer, we decided that next year we too would do our own grand tour. We too would ride into Paris, in our case from London, and for good measure we would ride back as well. The idea for the Tour Hi-Secure (the name of my brother's

London–based security business) was born over that weekend and it was to become a goal for which I could train, and an adventure for which we could plan.

It was Monday and as I sat in the departure lounge at Charles de Gaulle airport waiting for my flight back to Liverpool, I became aware of a group of twenty or so Australians mulling around the terminal. I could not explain their presence and the penny only started to drop when it became clear to me that they too were booked onto the Liverpool flight. It must be something to do with Manchester and the Commonwealths, I thought. The Games were now in full swing back in my home town. My suspicions were confirmed when a middle-aged couple sat down next to me on the flight and seeing my cycling magazine they began to enquire about the results of the cycling events in the Games. I answered with what information I had and as we spoke it became apparent that the couple were in some way related to an Australian cyclist. The questions though were 'how' and 'who'.

The answers came soon enough; the couple were in fact the parents of Bradley McGee, a hugely talented professional rider from the Française des Jeux team (or as they referred to it FDJ) which is sponsored by the French National Lottery. Their son had just completed the Tour, with the added honour of actually having won the stage into Avranche. They were now heading to Manchester to watch him compete in perhaps his most favoured discipline, the four-kilometre track pursuit. This is a race in which two riders begin on opposite sides of the track, with the aim of chasing (or pursuing) each other over the distance of the race. Accompanying Mr and Mrs McGee, but dotted around the plane, were one of Bradley's brothers and his own wife and young child. The other Australians on the flight were mainly family members of other bike riders that were taking part in the Games, who had stopped over in Paris on their way to Manchester.

For the hour of the flight Mr and Mrs McGee proved to be warm and friendly and we talked about Bradley's struggles and achievements both in the Tour, but also at earlier stages in his career. A talented track rider, after completing high-school he had been enrolled at the Australian Institute of Sport, something of a hothouse environment for young high-achievers in many sports from across the whole country. Following this, he had enjoyed success on the track at world level, before earning a professional contract with FDJ. Bradley was also at the forefront of a more generalised boom in the Australian presence in the professional peloton and within his own team he was joined by other countrymen in the form of Baden Cooke and Matthew Wilson.

In the short time we were together we talked about other subjects as well as cycling and on the way discovered a shared love of rugby league. As Sydneysiders, it was not a surprise to find that the McGees (Brad included) were avid fans and we talked about the poor season which their team, the Parramatta Eels, was having back home. Perhaps the most significant comment though came from Johnny McGee (Bradley's Dad) who pronounced that not only was Bradley a champion cyclist, he was also a champion son. You could almost touch the pride that the McGees had for their son; something that I was to see again on live TV only a few days later.

This triggered another string of questions in my head. What do professional cyclists do when not riding their bikes? What kind of people are they? Is there such a thing as a typical top-level bike rider? Do they even have time for other interests?

I said my goodbyes to the McGee family as we touched down at Liverpool's John Lennon airport, conscious that the experience of meeting them, though brief, was likely to be a further spur to my inquisitiveness. It was another message telling me to find out more and to get to the bottom of the riddle of Philip Evans.

Back home and having made a note of the date and time of the four-kilometre pursuit, I sat back to watch the TV coverage of the Games. Bradley McGee had made it to the final with ease and he was up against Bradley Wiggins, who was representing England. Both Brads were members of the FDJ team, but for now at least national identity took precedence over team loyalties. In an incredible ride McGee actually caught Wiggins, something that is rarely seen in top-level pursuiting, to claim the gold medal for Australia. It was a truly awesome performance from a man that had been seemingly made stronger for the experience of riding the Tour de France and I must admit to actually having cheered for an Australian against a Briton for perhaps the one and only time in my life.

Track bikes have a single fixed gear and no brakes. As a result, the only way that the riders can slow down is to pedal progressively more slowly as they circle the track. After a few laps of slowing down McGee moved up the banking and came to a halt on the finishing straight. Holding onto the safety rail with one hand, he proceeded to embrace his Mum and Dad who were watching from the front row. It was a sweet moment and in some small and voyeuristic way, I felt part of it.

I have continued to follow Bradley McGee's increasingly successful career since this time and when in 2003 he took the yellow jersey after the prologue time trial of the centenary Tour de France it was his proud parents back in Australia that I thought of.

By 2003 my illness was only a bad memory and having managed to shift most of my excess weight and regained my fitness I was, approximately one year behind schedule, finally ready to join a cycling club. After making a number of enquiries, I decided to join one of the best-known clubs in the area, ABC Centreville. The club enjoys a good reputation within the sport and has a record of producing riders of good repute, including a British female world champion in Mandy Jones. If anything, I was worried that the standard within the club would be too good for me and it was something of a leap into the unknown. However, since being ill I had become much more likely to take a chance and so it was on Sunday January 19th that I undertook my first organised ride with the club; some 60 miles up and down the West Pennine Moors of Lancashire. The participants were to ride in two groups: the first slow group, comprising one or two senior riders, there mainly to accompany juniors and novices such as myself, and then one hour later a second group of more experienced and quicker riders. The ride with the slow group was thankfully at a pace that I could maintain, but after around 50 miles the riders from the first group began to stream past us at some speed. My competitive instincts meant that I did my best to keep up with them, but it was not long before they disappeared into the distance. I was particularly interested, not to say, embarrassed, to note that one of the riders that left me behind was not even riding a road bike, preferring instead to use a heavy mountain bike. I did not know it at the time, but the man on the mountain bike was Phil Evans.

What serendipity. I remember soon after that first ride casually asking one of my new-found club-mates if they knew of a rider called Philip Evans, only to be told that prior to embarking on his adventure in France, Phil, or to give him his more familiar name, Cheeky Phil, had himself been a member of the very same ABC Centreville club. A promising rider in the UK, he had just missed out on selection for the Great Britain squad and instead had decided to further his career by riding in France, where he was being supported by a body called the Dave Rayner Fund.

Cheeky Phil was back home from France, where he now spent most of his year, for a winter visit and had been out with his former club that day. I was told he had ridden past me somewhere near Tescos supermarket in Bury with some of his old friends from the Manchester Velodrome. This was hard to comprehend. In fact it still is. The figure in the UC Briquebec shirt at the Nationals and the man on the yellow mountain bike that cold, wet day in Bury were one and the same. The notion of exploring the lives of young British riders in Europe now developed a momentum of its own. Rather than being something that I wanted to do, the project was becoming something that I had to undertake. It was driving me rather than the other way around.

By the time I became aware of the remarkable coincidence of Cheeky Phil, I had missed the opportunity to meet him, as he had headed back to France to commence his preparations for the forthcoming season. However, although we had not yet met, Phil's story was continuing to exert a great influence upon me. At the same time I was becoming anxious to find out more about the Dave Rayner Fund. What was this body? How and why did they support riders? I remembered that there was a professional cyclist of that name some years before, but did not yet know how his name had come to be associated with a group that helped young cyclists in this way.

It was now Easter 2003 and Julia and I ventured back to Normandy for another holiday in the area, staying as we always do in the quiet and largely undiscovered twin seaside towns of Barneville-Carteret, some 15 kilometres west of Briquebec. We never anticipated becoming the kind of people who go back to the same place year on year. However, since our first visit we had become so besotted with Barneville that we could not contemplate a year without the thought of our annual pilgrimage. In fact, the area holds such a special place in our hearts, with its relaxed pace of life and dramatic views, that are illuminated at night by the lighthouse which stands atop the Cap D'Carteret, that it is with some reluctance that I even give out its name, save it will be discovered by too many people.

I took my bike with me on the holiday, and whilst we were in Barneville I undertook a number of rides, half hoping each time I was out to find myself on the same road as Cheeky Phil and his UC Briquebec teammates. This did not happen, but one day we picked up a local French newspaper to see a headline proclaiming Phil's success in a significant race that had taken place over the Easter weekend. Without even meeting our paths had crossed once again. However, what we didn't know at the time was just how close we had come to our first encounter, because Phil was actually living in a flat on the seafront of Barneville-Carteret at the time of our visit.

By the summer I had done my research on the Dave Rayner Fund. I had found that it had been set up in the aftermath of the death of a British professional rider and that its main aim was to help support young British riders that had chosen to live and compete on the continent. Once more deciding that it is always best to take a chance, I decided to approach the Fund directly in an attempt to gain their backing for my project. The aim would be to follow one or more riders, through the 2004 season, through the various ups and the downs that they experienced, both on the bike and off. The support of the Fund would provide a great boost to the project and the whole thing was much more likely to be successful with their help. In return

I hoped that my efforts would in some small way help to heighten its profile and if possible also do something to swell its coffers.

After writing an introductory letter to the Chairman of the Fund, Dudley Hayton, I was able to arrange an introductory meeting with three of its Trustees. It was on a warm summer night in July 2003 that I pitched the story of Cheeky Phil to them. Looking back at me in the room that night were Dudley Hayton, Bill Holmes and Keith Lambert. Familiar names to fans of cycling and men who were among the premier UK bike riders of the respective generations. Although they were friendly to me, the experience of explaining my plans and justifying my intentions was more nerve wracking than any job interview. I had to quickly establish my credentials with these men, both as a serious writer and also as someone who could be trusted with a small part of the memory of their departed friend. In a sense I also had to sell to them the notion of a relative newcomer like myself having access to some of the most interesting inner-workings of the sport, but I was lucky that night and they saw something that made them think it was worthwhile taking a risk and backing me. The idea was accepted in principle and my need to learn about the lifestyle of the young elite bike rider was now likely to be satisfied. After some pleasantries and conscious of over-staying my welcome I made my excuses and drove home and into a beautiful sunset. A major hurdle had been negotiated and I felt excited and relieved. However, when I awoke on the following day, a new weight of responsibility had fallen upon me. I realised that the Dave Rayner Fund had now made a commitment to me and I had to show dedication, organisation and some talent too, in order to return it.

What follows is the story of the period between my initial meeting with the representatives of the Dave Rayner Fund and the start of 2005. It portrays the lives and cycling experiences of two of the crop of 2004 and attempts to shed light on the ethos and workings of the Fund itself. It is about what it takes to succeed in cycling and the sacrifices that aspiring sportsmen and women are prepared to make to reach their goal. It is also about success and failure and encompasses both tragedy and joy.

Perhaps more than this though, it is about people and the journeys they have to make. It portrays a series of different personal and professional odysseys that took place over this period: those of the riders that I followed, that of the Fund itself, my own and not least that of the seemingly ubiquitous Cheeky Phil Evans.

CHAPTER 2

The Dave Rayner Fund

IF I CAME TO the Dave Rayner Fund in a state of joyfulness, the origins of the Fund itself could not have been more different. It was formed in early 1995, after the death in November of the previous year of the young man after which the body was to take its name.

Dave Rayner was born in Shipley, West Yorkshire in March 1967, the son of John and Barbara. Cycling was integral to the family and John Rayner was himself a first category racing cyclist. It was no surprise that Dave joined his first club, East Bradford CC, as a 12-year-old. Showing a prodigious talent from an early age, Dave moved to the higher profile Bradford Wheelers and in his first significant victory, claimed the National Junior road race title at Stoke on Trent. In 1984, and at the age of 17, Dave took the opportunity to further his ambitions by going to ride in Italy for the GS Porcari-Fanini-Berti team. This brought him into contact with and into competition with the best Italian riders of that generation, one that included the likes of Mario Cipollini and Andrea Tafi. Dave stayed in Italy until the end of 1986 and his spell there undoubtedly helped him to develop as a rider. In 1985, for example, he came 14th in the Junior World Road Race and 5th in the World Junior Team Time Trial.

In 1987 he went on to take the under-22 award in the famous Milk Race, whilst still an amateur. However, the lure of the paid ranks and his desire to turn cycling into a fully-fledged career, meant that Dave was to turn professional. By 1988 he was riding for the top British team of the day, Raleigh-Banana and again he won the under-22 award in the Milk Race (at the same time taking 8th overall). He repeated the feat in 1989, but with the British professional scene entering the doldrums at the end of the decade, Dave was lucky enough to join the Dutch Buckler team. After two successful years of top-level continental racing, Dave moved countries once more, this time going to the USA, where in 1993 he rode for IME-Health Share.

Despite his somewhat itinerant lifestyle, Dave found the time to fall in love, and he returned to Bradford to be married to Serena. In 1994 he rode in the UK for the Lex Townsend team. This, however, was to be his last season. In November of that year he was enjoying an off-season night out with friends in Bradford. The evening was to end in despair however, as an incident outside a nightclub left Dave in a critical condition in a local hospital. Tragically, he was not to pull through.

The notion of forming the Fund came about on the day that Dave's all too short life was brought to an end. The idea took shape as Dudley Hayton and Colin Willcock travelled from Bradford to Manchester along the M62 motorway. At the time, Dudley was the manager of Dave's Lex Townsend team and had been due to take him that evening to the track league at the newly-opened indoor Velodrome in the city. Having visited Dave twice at Bradford Royal Infirmary hospital that day though, he knew that the doctors were now planning to switch off his life support machine.

The trip to Manchester was still made. Partly as a mark of respect to Dave and also to break the awful news to his friends. During their 30-odd-mile journey across the Pennines, Dudley told Colin of his need to do something for Dave and his family. Dudley said that he wanted to start a Fund in Dave's name and asked Colin for his thoughts on what the best purpose for this could be. After some thought, Colin suggested that it should be to help young riders to race in Europe. As they knew, Dave had gone to Italy, with the support of his parents, whilst still in his teens and this had helped to make him as a bike rider. Such an idea would be a fitting tribute to their friend.

A week or so later, and with Dave's death still at the forefront of everyone's mind, Dudley and Colin sat down to put together a list of names of people who knew and admired Dave and who would be interested in being part of the Committee of the new Dave Rayner Fund. That list included Graham Baxter, Bill Holmes, Bernard Burns, Alan Rushton, Keith Lambert, Jonny Clay, Sid Barras and Gary Rayner (Dave's brother) and all were in attendance on 12th January 1995, when the Fund met for the first time at the Richardsons Arms, in Bradford. At the meeting Dudley Hayton was elected to the role of Chairman and Colin became the Secretary, roles that they still fulfil today. At the meeting the main objective of the Fund was also agreed to be:

> to enable a promising young rider to spend some time abroad developing his talents in a true racing environment, much as Dave Rayner's trip to Italy helped him develop into one of the country's top riders.

However, one of the first acts of the Fund was to pay for an engraved seat and stone to be placed on the banks of the river Aire at Gargrave. The memorial to Dave remains in place today and anyone visiting that small village in the heart of the Yorkshire Dales can easily find it and spend a few quiet moments of contemplation. Gargrave is a favourite stopping off point for all kinds of cyclists and also formed part of one of Dave's regular training runs. Pass 'The Dalesman' tea-shop on any Sunday and you will see a plethora of all kinds of bicycles stacked outside, whilst inside you will hear bike-riders from all parts of Yorkshire and Lancashire enjoying the craic.

The men that came together that sad night in Bradford were Dave's mentors and peers and almost without exception were Yorkshiremen too. In addition, they were all past or current professional road-racers of some renown. In fact, the present Committee of the Fund reads like a who's who of British road racing over the past four decades and such factors have played a major role in shaping the aims as well as the character of the organisation.

Derek Smith, for example, won over 200 races during an

illustrious career that began in the 1950s, including 6 National Road Race titles. Similarly, Bernard Burns turned professional at the tender age of 19, before going on race in France and the United Kingdom for a number of well-respected teams, such as Viking and Falcon. After numerous high finishes in the National Road Race, including a second place, Bernard turned his hand to coaching and was for a time the British Cycling Federations National Coach. Bernard played a key role in the early career of Dave, and it was he who helped to engineer the opportunity for Dave to go to Italy. Bill Holmes is the Treasurer of the Fund. After representing Great Britain at the Melbourne Olympics of 1956 (where he shared a room with Tom Simpson), Bill went on to have a successful career on the road, both as an amateur and a professional.

Three of the long-term stalwarts of the Fund came from the next generation of top British riders. Keith Lambert, Sid Barras and Dudley Hayton rode with and against each other at the top level in the late 1970s and 1980s. Dudley himself was a regular on the podium in the National Road Race before going on to enjoy a career in team management. Keith 'Legs' Lambert's achievements included 3 overall wins in the Milk Race and 2 National Road Race titles. Keith also enjoyed successes in important stage races in Europe and Australasia and he too went into the management side of cycling, working with a number of teams. 'Super' Sid Barras was a prodigious winner of road races during a long career that lasted from the late 1960s to the mid 1980s. In addition, Sid's career included a season spent riding at the very top level for the TI Raleigh team, which as with Dave's Buckler team was based in Holland.

A third group involved with the Fund came from Dave's own generation. Johnny Clay counted Dave as both a close friend and a colleague and as a youngster he too went abroad, riding in France in 1984 and 1985. As late as 2000 Johnny was winning the bronze medal as part of the British four-kilolmetre pursuit team at the Sydney Olympics, as well as the silver medal in the same event at the World Championships. Likewise, Chris Walker won National Junior titles in 1982 and 1983 and in 1984 he too lived and raced in Italy. After turning professional,

Chris went on to ride for a number of teams in the UK and in the USA and in 1984 was a team-mate of Dave's with Lex Townsend.

As can be seen, many of the Fund's Committee members had lived the life of the continental cyclist at some stage of their own career. Indeed, the trek from Britain to Europe has long been seen as an integral part of the quest for cycling success. But why is this? The answer is that Europe is a tougher and more competitive environment in which to race than Britain and this is where an ambitious young rider has to serve their apprenticeship on the road to becoming a fully developed rider. To put it another way, Europe is where the action is, both in terms of the level of the racing experience, but also in the pursuit of a coveted professional contract. Today, the United Kingdom supports only a handful of professional teams, and sadly none of them rival the size and financial clout of those in countries such as France, Belgium, Spain and Italy. From time to time a new ambitious set-up will emerge in Britain (the ill-fated Linda McCartney team was perhaps the last of these), but unfortunately more often than not they fail amid acrimony and unpaid wages. Therefore in the majority of cases, if a rider is to reach the top of their profession, it is much more than likely to be done in Europe than at home in the UK.

The Fund realised early on that if it was to maintain an ongoing commitment to young riders, it would have to be skilled in fund-raising. Over the years this has developed into a well-managed enterprise and a number of events throughout the course of the year help to keep the bank balance healthy. Unsolicited donations are one source of income. These vary in size, but in all cases are examples of individuals, clubs or other bodies simply wishing to show their support of the Fund and its aims. Some of the donations are sent as bequests and it is an indication of the warmth with which the Fund is regarded, that even in their own time of loss, people are able to find the time to help the organisation. Another source of income is the annual 'Rayner's Ride', which took place for a number of years in early October. The ride, which is open to all, begins in the North Yorkshire market town of Skipton and takes a route through the quiet country lanes of the Dales, before ending near the site of the memorial to Dave in Gargrave.

Perhaps the most important fund-raiser, though, is the Dave Rayner Fund Memorial Dinner. Held annually in November, the dinner has grown into one of 'the' events on the British cycling calendar. Indeed, such is its stature today, that the guest of honour at the 2003 dinner was none other than Miguel Indurain, the five-time winner of the Tour de France. It was no surprise that the 600 tickets for the event sold out within weeks and that the dinner went on to raise in the region of £27,000. Part of this came from an auction of a variety of desirable items such as a Real Madrid shirt signed by David Beckham and David Millar's recently gained World Champions jersey. Anyone hoping for a ticket for the 2004 dinner was also likely to be disappointed as the dinner sold out again, this time before the end of 2003.

In addition to the visit in 2003 of a cycling legend, the dinner is regularly graced by the presence of Olympians and other high-class track and road cyclists from Britain and abroad. Regular attendees, for example, have included Chris Boardman and Jason Queally who won Gold on the track for Britain at the Barcelona and Sydney games respectively. Also, a number of the current riders attend the dinner and are presented to the guests. For the paying public, it is a night to remember, but for its organisers the evening is one of work more than play.

Such tireless effort by the Committee of the Fund has the aim of raising money to support a group of gifted young cyclists; but how are the individual riders chosen? The process begins before the dinner when prospective beneficiaries are asked via the cycling press to submit their CVs. These take a variety of forms and vary in style and quality in the same way as do the riders themselves. In normal circumstances the Fund will support a rider for up to three years and so in every batch of applications there will be some existing supported riders. Also, in most years a number of the candidates stand out for selection. These will often be juniors that have a certain pedigree and who have already been successful at a national level. Others though, will be new names to the selection panel and they will be the main subjects of a series of, sometimes heated, discussions.

Once the decisions have been made on whom to support, the emphasis turns to the logistics of the operation. For example, some of the riders will already have placements arranged with amateur clubs on the continent, but sometimes the men behind the Fund will have to use their extensive network of contacts to help the riders to find a club. Also, the level of the practical help required will be influenced by what the rider's new team are able to offer. Some more affluent clubs (perhaps with sponsorship in place) are able to offer accommodation, equipment, a job and even expenses. However, this is not always the case and it really is a case of the luck of the draw for the riders, as to how well they will be looked after. Obviously the more a club can offer, the less that a rider will need from the Fund. Whatever the level of support required, however, once in situ the riders (and some eighteen were helped in 2003) will receive monthly allowances.

In addition to the regular rider's cheques, the Fund may also give one-off payments or provide equipment, should for instance a rider damage his bike in a crash. This in fact happened to Phil Evans in 2003 after he experienced a particularly nasty accident during a race in Switzerland. Descending a mountain, Phil came round a sharp bend only to find a parked car on the road. It was too late for evasive action and Phil ploughed into the car, seriously injuring himself and wrecking his bike at the same time. Luckily the Fund was on hand to supply him with replacement equipment, even if they could not do much to heal the many cuts and bruises that he suffered in the incident.

In exchange for the support of the Fund, the riders are expected to maintain regular contact with their supporters back in the UK. This is done through Keith Lambert, who acts as Rider Liaison Officer. Keith makes and takes phone calls, as well as exchanging emails with the riders. His main concern is the general welfare of his charges, but he is also very interested in how they are faring in competition. Some riders are more communicative than others and also the experience of new cultures and surroundings differs from one to the next. The young men (and now also the women) who venture abroad are likely to have a new language to learn, new customs to adapt to and they may also face the prospect of being away from home for the first time. As a result, it is not a surprise that each year a small number of the riders quickly decide that the life of an elite European cyclist is not for them. Some thus return home in mid-season and in fact the selection process takes into account a degree of attrition amongst those that are chosen. On the other hand, nothing succeeds like success and every good result for a Dave Rayner Fund rider has a positive effect on the organisation as a whole and it is useful that a number of graduates of the Fund, such as Charlie Wegelius and Jamie Burrow, have gone on to earn professional contracts.

The success of the 2003 Dave Rayner dinner and the attendance of 'Big Mig' helped to raise the profile of the Fund to a much higher level. When I met Dudley, Keith and Bill for the first time I was aware that the organisation was entering a transitional phase. One in which the efforts of earlier years were beginning to bear fruit. This meant that more money was coming in and more riders could be supported, but also that the effort required to administer the Fund was growing at a rapid rate. Put simply, there was a danger that the Fund would become the victim of its own success. This has certainly become the case with the annual dinner and such is the demand for tickets today that each year sees an ever-growing number of disappointed potential supporters. The room used at the Bradford Hilton hotel holds some 600 diners, but is simply not big enough to accommodate all those who would like to attend.

Now that the Fund is in a position to support more riders than ever before, the challenge is to unearth the next big thing. This is a pressure keenly felt by the Committee members. At the same time the image of the Fund is of immense importance to those involved. Central to all decision making is the need to maintain a reputation that does justice to the memory of Dave Rayner. To an extent this sets the Fund aside from other bodies. Also, it should be remembered that the Fund is a charity that relies solely on the effort of volunteers. In fact, it is only the hard work of Dudley and the others that stands between young riders living the dream of the continental professional, or being forced to remain in the relative backwater of domestic cycling. When the dust had settled on my first meeting with Bill, Keith and

Dudley I was aware that I now too shared some of this responsibility. I was, whether I liked it or not, now an advocate for the Fund.

Although my first steps on the road to forging a link with the Fund had been taken in high summer, in reality the project would only move ahead when the riders to be supported in 2004 had been chosen. It was therefore unsurprising that there was a lull between the months of August and October. However, I received a call from Dudley in mid-November that left me very excited. I had been asked to attend the rider selection meeting. I was to see how the young men would be chosen and this seemed like an act of real acceptance. I was unaware at the time, however, that I had misinterpreted the invitation and that my lesson in responsibility was soon to be replayed, but this time before a larger and somewhat more intimidating audience – the full Committee of the Fund.

CHAPTER 3

Natural Selection

THE MORNING OF Sunday 30th November 2003 dawned bright and cold. It was tailor made for a leisurely off-season ride, but on this particular morning the Committee members of the Dave Rayner Fund would not get out on their bikes. Instead, they were driving to the Hilton Hotel in Bradford to select the riders that they would support in 2004. I too was on my to Bradford, thinking that I was about to sit in on one of the most important meetings that I would attend all year. However, things were not to quite work out that way.

In my eagerness I set off early and I was in fact the first to arrive at the hotel. I watched as one by one the key men involved with the Fund began to appear. I had already met Dudley, Keith and Bill and had been introduced to Bernard Burns and Derek Smith at the Rayner's Ride in October. However, this meeting was my first introduction to the Committee as a whole and as they discussed the previous day's football results there was a definite sense of there being an interloper in the room and that the offender was me.

As we waited for a conference suite to be made ready for us, talk turned to the imminent demise of the Life Repair team. This had been the premier professional team in the UK in 2003 and had on its roster a number of the 'big-hitters' of the domestic scene in John Tanner, Mark Lovatt and Kevin Dawson. Life Repair was managed by Dr Phil Leigh, a well-known face on the

UK scene, and was backed by the Lancaster-based claims and compensation service which gave the team its name. Dr Leigh had well-publicised intentions to grow the team over a number of years and to expand its calendar so that it would compete in significant races on the continent. However, the company had suffered a downturn in its fortunes in the general backlash against the claims culture and after experiencing financial difficulties it had gone into liquidation, leading to a loss of jobs and also to the end of the cycling team. At the same time, Sid Barras had to report that his son Tom, who had been supported by the Fund over a number of years, had been let down over a professional contract with a team in Belgium and was now looking for a last minute alternative ride for 2004. Both stories, although disappointing, were typical of the vagaries of the life of the cyclist. Promises are often made, but for one reason or another, they do not always turn into something concrete. What I didn't know at the time of the meeting was that the two events under discussion that morning would exert a great influence on the riders that I was to follow in 2004.

The use of a conference suite in a large hotel for the annual selection meeting was something of a departure for the Fund. In previous years such meetings took place in smoky pub rooms in and around Bradford. There was even a time in the early days when all the prospective riders would be interviewed in person as part of the process. Now however, the number of CVs submitted and the need to do equal justice to each applicant meant that it was no longer feasible to do this. To me this was another indication of an organisation in a period of change. The success of the Fund was breeding a new set of demands, hence the need for greater formality, for example in selecting riders.

Once up in the conference room it quickly became clear to me that not everyone was entirely comfortable with my presence. After one or two half-whispered questions regarding who I was and why I was there, it was made clear to me that I would not be staying for the selection meeting proper and that any questions about how riders are selected and as importantly, on what criteria the unsuccessful ones are overlooked, would not be welcomed. This, I guessed, was a reaction to some bad post-selection reactions in the past and with hindsight was an entirely understandable stance. However, at the time it felt like the rug had been pulled from under me and left me with limited room for manoeuvre. Unprepared as I was, I had to think on my feet. Clearly flustered I asked the Committee a series of general questions about their own cycling careers, their experiences on the Continent and the general aims of the Fund. Over the next thirty minutes, however, I was able to tease out their views and opinions on wider range of issues stretching from the quality of the riders that apply to the Fund, through to the challenges faced by a foreigner riding for a continental team and on to the general politics of the sport in Britain. I have to admit though that this was more a product of their enthusiasm and eagerness to talk than of my own interviewing skills.

One particular question I asked was about the aims of the Fund and why it had not formed its own team or actually bought a house in France or Belgium where the chosen riders could live together, such as had been done in the past by the Australian and Irish governing bodies. This in some ways seemed like a logical progression for the Fund and it had been considered at some points in the past. However, the idea had always ultimately been rejected and the reason given was that with their background in team management, people like Dudley and Keith appreciated just how great a logistical and administrative burden this would be. Instead, it was thought more effective for the Fund to offer backing and support, whilst at the same time placing the onus for success and failure on the shoulders of the riders themselves. Also, the approach of placing riders within clubs would help to develop their ability to cope with the uncertain life of a full-time bike rider. It was thought that the independence and self-reliance which is crucial to dealing with the demands placed upon professional sportsmen and women would be more likely to flourish if the riders had to fend for themselves.

Another thing to strike me during the meeting was the prickly nature of the relationship between the Fund and the British Cycling Federation, the sport's governing body in the UK. I was sad to realise that in some ways the two bodies are at odds and in competition with each other for talent. It was likely, for example, that some of the riders that had applied for support from the Fund would also at some point have had been in contact with the talent-spotters from the BCF. Also, the BCF was perceived as concentrating too much on the nurturing of talent on the track rather than in supporting and developing road racing in the UK. Differences in ethos were also apparent, stemming in part from the fact the Fund is a voluntary body, whilst the BCF is staffed by paid employees. On first impressions it was also apparent that in some ways the Fund represented the old school of cycling coaching and the development of talent, whilst on the other hand the BCF is seen to be more science-based in its approach.

As I outlined my proposal to the group, Sid Barras made an aside on the pressures he was under when riding for the famous Dutch team manager Peter Post as part of the TI Raleigh team, and what an added and unnecessary burden it would have been to be followed around by a writer. This was meant as a throwaway comment, but it told me something about one of the potential issues I would face and also the nature of my relationship with the riders that I would follow. Being the subject of a book could bring positive publicity to the young men and in that respect it held attractions. However, it would also mean pulling back the curtain even in a small way on an otherwise closed world and it meant that I would see them when they were possibly unhappy or struggling to cope.

Obviously the subject of drugs could also form part of this and I knew even at this early stage that I had a decision to make. Books such as 'Breaking the Chain' by the Belgian 'soigneur' Willy Voet (a soigneur carries out a number of roles in a team such as preparing food and giving massages and in Voet's case administering the team's supply of performance-enhancing drugs) and the award winning 'A Rough Ride', by the Irish cyclist and writer Paul Kimmage, have done much to lift the lid on the nefarious practices that go on in the professional peloton, and before commencing the undertaking, I thought long and hard about this element of the sport and what my approach to it would be. In the end I concluded that the book had not been conceived as an exposé on drugs in sport and so would not be an exploration of the subject to the detriment of other elements of cycling. I was more interested in the dream of making it in cycling than in the nightmare of drugs in sport. I also figured that whatever illegal sacrifices bike riders make in this pursuit, they ultimately have their own consciences and health to answer to, rather than my own moral judgements. However, at the same time I decided that if anything came up in this area during the course of the year I would not and could not shy away from dealing with it.

When my allotted time was up I thanked the Committee and left them to go through the CVs. I travelled back in more sunshine and on arriving home jumped on my bike for a few priceless hours riding and reflection on the morning's events.

Then on 5th December 2003, I received an email on behalf of the Committee of the Fund. This was in the form of a Press Release, announcing that they had received CVs from a total of 43 riders requiring assistance for the 2004 racing season and that from this group they had selected 23 riders to support. This was a record number, made possible in no small part by the success of the annual dinner. The list was:

1. Jamie Alberts (Chesterfield)
2. Yanto Barker (Devon)
3. Tom Barras (Keighley)
4. Graham Briggs (Doncaster)
5. David Clarke (Derbyshire)
6. Ryan Connor (Ballymena, N. Ireland)
7. Alex Coutts (Midlothian, Scotland)
8. Chris Daddy (Hull)
9. James Flanagan (Leighton Buzzard)
10. Daniel Fleeman (Burton on Trent)
11. Adam Illingworth (Aylesbury)
12. Andy Jackson (Cleveland)
13. Steve Lampier (Helston)
14. Dan Lloyd (Dorset)
15. James Millard (Guildford)
16. Andrew Murphy (Fife, Scotland)
17. Paidi O'Brien (Cork, Ireland)
18. Chris Penketh (Merseyside)
19. Jon Rutherford (Sheffield)
20. David Smith (Caithness, Scotland)
21. Tom Southam (Penzance)
22. James Stewart (Ormskirk)
23. James Williamson (Crewe)

I studied the list and without knowing any of the individual riders, considered who would be the ones to work with. There were a number of issues to consider, such as the optimum number of stories to tell and the best combination of riders and locations. However, before Keith Lambert could let me have his even suggestions on behalf of the Fund, the lucky individuals had to be contacted and to give their response to the offer of support. I spoke to Keith and agreed that we would leave things to work themselves out over the next few weeks and that we would talk again in early 2004, once the final list was clear.

Christmas came and went and I grew expectant waiting for Keith's call. When it came, he gave me the names of Tom Barras and Graham Briggs as the 'lucky' young men that would be the recipients of my attention throughout 2004. So, who were my new friends?

24-year-old Tom is the son of Sid and like Dave Rayner himself, has cycling in his blood. After completing a degree at Loughborough University, he had hoped to join the Linda McCartney team, but with its demise he went to Belgium instead where he joined the newly formed Team Down Under organisation. Originally run on an amateur basis, Team Down Under had risen through the ranks to become a semi-professional division-three trade team. Although managed by two Belgians, Gilbert de Weerdt and Rudi Dubois, the team was staffed mainly with young Australian riders and acted as a platform for aspiring young cyclists, with at least one (Matt Wilson) going on to ride for a big team, in the form of Brad McGee's FDJ.com organisation. The unusual nature of the team often enabled it to gain rides in significant races throughout the season, which were a showcase for the riders to prove that they could compete on a higher level. Tom was about to embark on his fourth year with the team and was one of only four non-Australians, the others being another Briton, Hamish Haynes, together with two Belgian riders. Also, for 2004 the team had received sponsorship from an Australian cycling website and so had undergone a name change to Cyclingnews.com.

Graham Briggs was the reigning British age group time-trial champion, and younger at just 20. He was about to begin his first year on the continent, having gained a ride with the amateur UC Beauvais Oise club in northern France. Interestingly, he had no family connection with cycling and had come to it by himself, first as a mountain biker and then as a road racer. Initially he had been hoping to gain a place on the newly formed British Cycling Federation Under-23 Endurance Squad, but had been informed just before Christmas that he had not been successful. So instead he had to make his own arrangements for 2004 and although he had been a member of the Life Repair team in 2003, this option had disappeared together with the team itself late in the year. The ride with the Beauvais club had come about at short notice and somewhat fortuitously, after another foreign rider had accepted and then ultimately turned down the opportunity to ride for the club.

Keith's suggestions seemed to me good ones. The contrast in background, ages and levels of experience between the two young men would be likely to lead to two distinct storylines. In addition, their respective home towns of Keighley and Doncaster were easily accessible to me, as would be their summer bases in Belgium and France. All in all, it seemed a logical choice and excitedly I set about making arrangements for my first meeting with the two. However, before doing this I finally had the chance to meet Phil Evans and again it was something that owed much to chance.

It was January when I made a casual remark to one of my own clubmates at ABC Centreville about the whereabouts and fortunes of Phil. I knew that in past years he had returned to the UK early in the year and sometimes had even attended the Centreville Club Dinner. However, I was even more surprised to be told, 'You're in luck – he's back from France for a week with his girlfriend. He's staying with his parents and here's the phone number.' 'What? Right now?' I thought and I clearly remember the nerves I felt when ringing the number late one Sunday evening. Luckily Phil was immediately friendly and it seemed that someone at the club may have already told him to expect a call from me. We arranged to meet at 5pm on the following Friday at the Manchester Velodrome, where his Mum forms part of the hardworking staff. During the week my sense of anticipation grew until I left work early that day to make a mad dash to Manchester. On my arrival I was slightly taken aback by the number of cars and amount of activity going on. It seemed that the Velodrome, which is part of a much larger sporting complex built to host the Commonwealth Games, was being used as a venue for the National Badminton championships. As I entered the building the thought struck me that many of my dreams and aspirations were in the process of coming together and I was on the verge of meeting someone that had become something of an unknowing inspiration to me. The realisation of a dream, even in a small way, can be an intimidating proposition, but luckily I managed to retain a veneer of calm as I met firstly Phil's Mum and then the man himself. I recounted the story of Rivington and its aftermath once more and although frequency of repetition meant that I was becoming a more practised storyteller, it felt very different to be explaining myself at last to its main subject.

Due to the badminton tournament we had been forced to conduct our conversation in one of the darkened bar areas away from the main hall of the building and our surroundings only added to the sense of the surreal that pervaded the meeting. Taking to Phil in the twilight and asking him about his introduction to the sport, how and when he had joined Centreville and how this had led him ultimately to France; all the time with his answers being interspersed with applause from the badminton spectators only yards away, made for a most unusual conversation. However, I was struck by his enthusiasm for the project and sense of community with other bike riders.

I was particularly interested in Phil's experiences in France and thought that they would give me an insight into some of the issues that would be faced by Tom and Graham. Phil's first year had been spent in the industrial town of Evreaux in the northern part of Normandy. This had been a (not always pleasant) learning experience for him as he faced the challenges of living away from home, sharing a non-too plush team house with erstwhile strangers (his main co-habitee was a young rider from Poland) and learning a new language. These factors contributed to an unspectacular first year, but buoyed by the support of the Fund and with a move to Briquebec things began to improve in his second season abroad. Phil was quick to draw the link between a happy and stable set of personal circumstances and success on the bike and he remained grateful to the French rider who had invited him to train and stay with him, to tend his garden and help keep the place in order. Following the move, Phil had begun to enjoy some success and 2003 brought a number of significant victories, including the one at Easter that I had read about in the press.

Latterly, the conversation moved on to his prospects for the coming year. Having been supported for three years by the Fund, Phil was going back to France, but was now faced with the prospect of working to make a living alongside his cycling. Such was the Evans family's gratitude though, that they had arranged an annual track meeting at the Velodrome, from which a proportion of the proceeds went to the Fund. Phil had now moved to the town of Avranche at the southernmost tip of Normandy, where he lived with his French girlfriend and where he was soon to start work in the town's Decathlon sports store. Cycling had led Phil to a new and different life, one that was far removed from the one that would have unfolded if he had stayed in England. In fact, Phil expressed such a love for the pace of life and the peace and scenery of Normandy, that it was hard to envisage him returning to the UK in the future and this was obviously something to which I could easily relate. We said our goodbyes and Phil told me that he was returning 'home' to France on the following day. Our meeting had lasted little more than an hour, but I felt that I had taken a major step forward, had managed to meet someone who had served as a totem for my recovery from illness and perhaps more importantly, I now had an inkling as to why everyone referred to Phil Evans as Cheeky Phil.

The firsts seemed to come thick and fast at this time and soon after I found myself on another evening drive, this time heading to Keighley to meet Tom and Graham for the first time. Having spoken with Phil, I had a clearer idea of what I wanted to achieve from the meeting. On a practical and factual level I wanted to find out as much as I could about the two, but more importantly I knew that I had to use the meeting to begin to build trust and a rapport between us. Honesty, I decided was the best way for me to do this. Once more I told my story and once more it sounded like an audition piece for a part in a show.

Tom and Graham listened while I spoke and then it was time to turn things around and ask them about themselves. This is not an easy situation and some people don't like to be in the spotlight. However, I managed to glean from Tom that his ambitions for the year were to win in Belgium, to do a big ride in the National Criterium Championships and to gain a stagiare contract. This is a short term trial at which a team can work with a rider and decide for themselves whether they think that they have the talent to make it with them.

As you might expect, Graham was much more circumspect on what lay before him, mainly because he didn't really know. He had never been to France before and did not really know where he was going and what was in store when he arrived. In terms of ambitions, he wanted simply to get through the year, but significantly he had earmarked the British Under-23 Road Race as a key target.

Both riders were due to go away on warm weather training camps before setting off for Belgium and France. Tom was going to work as a guide on an organised camp in Spain and this offered him the cost-free opportunity to get in the miles whilst the weather in the UK was at its worst. Graham on the other hand, was going to use money he had earned and saved whilst working over the winter to fund an independent trip to Tenerife.

I arranged to contact both Tom and Graham once they were in situ and after paying a visit to the bathroom, which typical of such a cycling-obsessed household had a gold-coloured Harrods team bike in the corner (Sid had been involved in the management of the short-lived team) I wished them well for the forthcoming weeks. As I made to leave I remember thinking that the two seemed to want to have a separate conversation without me around. This may have been harmless and may for example have been them merely catching up on mutual acquaintances.

However, as I closed the door I was aware that I had a long way to go to be fully part of this world. I was also aware that my cards were now on the table and I had an obligation to see the project through. It was early days, but like them, I felt a tinge of pressure to produce the goods.

CHAPTER 4

Graham Briggs, Premiere!

A **FEW WEEKS WENT** by following my first meeting with Graham and Tom. During that time Graham had travelled to France to join up with his new club, UC Beauvais, being met at Charles de Gaulle airport by his new team bosses before being taken to his new home in the town, some 50 kilometres north-west of Paris. Almost immediately though, he was dispatched to Toulon in the south of the country with the rest of the team for a training camp. Things did not begin auspiciously though, as the team coach broke down on the long drive back to Beauvais and the riders had to complete the journey by train. Unfortunately, the bikes stayed with the coach and the club missed the first weekend of the racing season as a result.

When competition did begin in early March, Graham took an encouraging 24th place in his first contest, an Elite open event in Belgium. He admitted to finding the race very fast, especially at the start, but he was strong enough to launch an attack near the end in an attempt to get across to the first break. This did not quite come off, but it was a solid start nevertheless, especially in view of the change and disruption that he had already experienced during his short time in France. However, even better news was soon to come.

I was keeping abreast of Graham's early progress and making arrangements for a first visit to him via his UK-based girlfriend

Samantha McInnes. Sam, who was emailing me updates of Graham's situation and early results whilst he was settling in, is of a similar age to Graham and the two have been together since they were 17. A trainee accountant by day, Sam was already Graham's unofficial press officer, photographer and agent in the UK and although she missed having him around, she was totally supportive of his decision to move to France to try to make it as a professional bike rider. The realisation of Graham's career aspirations was to be something of a team effort and I arranged through Sam that I would visit over the weekend of 12th and 13th March. As luck would have it, Sam had also arranged to pay Graham a visit over the same weekend. I booked flights and accommodation for myself and Julia, fully expecting this to be a low-key fact-finding visit to see how Graham was coming to terms with his new environment.

I didn't envisage that he would have any significant cycling experiences to talk about by the time of the visit and I was sanguine about this. However, my views underwent a sea change on 9th March when I read the result of the Paris–Evreux race on the British Cycling Federation website. There in first place was the name of Graham Briggs. Only two weeks after setting foot in the country and in his first major ride for the team, Graham had won one of the most prestigious events open to riders of his level in France. Paris–Evreux is roughly 100 miles in length and forms part of a series of highly significant races run throughout the season in towns around the French capital. It is open to riders up to and including only one level below the fully professional UCI (the governing body of world cycling) registered trade teams. Graham was the first UC Beauvais rider to win the race. In addition, the two previous British riders to achieve high finishes in Paris–Evreux were Robert Miller (who went on to have a highly successful professional career including winning the King of the Mountains competition in the Tour de France) and David Millar. This was a performance beyond all our expectations, with the possible exception of Sam, who had total belief in Graham's ability.

I emailed Sam once more, eager to learn more about the great news and she responded with an almost verbatim report from the victor of how he had jumped across to a break when the race went onto a small finishing circuit and how he had survived a front wheel puncture near the end to catch and pass the leaders for a clear victory by fifteen seconds. I was not altogether surprised when the same story appeared in a prominent position in the following week's edition of Cycling Weekly. This was Sam again, who had this time used her growing list of contacts within the cycling world to make sure that all the important people back home also got to hear the news of Graham's win.

This was now a great and thrilling context in which to be making our trip and we set off for Liverpool airport at 5.30am on Saturday 12th March bleary eyed, but at the same time very excited. Some hours later following the use of a car, an airliner and three trains we pulled into Beauvais. I remembered the town from the previous year when I had ridden from London to Paris with my brother and some friends. We had stopped in Beauvais for lunch on both our inbound and outbound journeys and had even watched the final rain soaked time trial of the Tour de France in a bar in the town. It struck me now, though, that for all the amusing anecdotes that I already had about this fairly anonymous provincial French town, another and more momentous story was in the process of being written.

Julia and I reached our hotel and waited for Graham and Sam's arrival at the agreed time of 2pm. Graham was not racing until Sunday and so this was an easy day for him in which he would ride for only a couple of hours in the morning with some of his team-mates. As the clock neared two, Julia asked me if I was nervous. Honestly, I had to answer yes. It wasn't every day that I travelled to France to interview an increasingly successful full-time cyclist about his life. What if he doesn't turn up, the doubting voices said, you'd look a fool. It was with relief therefore, that I shook Graham's hand at 2.01pm and offered him a drink after he had appeared in the foyer of the hotel. It wasn't Sam though that was with him, but instead he was accompanied by his team manager Laurent. Such was Graham's standing after the win that he had been chauffeured to our appointment, but unfortunately Laurent's small car was only capable of taking one passenger at a time and so Sam was back at the team house. We introduced ourselves to Laurent, who had a cheerful demeanour and who was clearly proud of his 'cycliste Anglais', but he spoke little English and Graham and I spoke little French. Julia was able to translate a little, but in our mutual nervousness we didn't realise that Laurent was explaining to us that he was going back to the team house to collect Samantha to bring her to the hotel too.

After Laurent left, we ordered coffees and sat down to find out how Graham was enjoying his new life. Things were a little stilted at first as one might expect, but we all relaxed as we started to talk about the race win. Paris–Evreux, we found out, was not an event that Graham had marked out as a target in his race calendar. In fact, he did not yet have his own copy of the team's itinerary for the season and was relying instead on borrowing copies from his team-mates. We were tasked with getting the only available version of the calendar photocopied for ourselves, but also for Graham too. In addition, he was so new to France that he had no idea where Evreux actually was, except that it was somewhere near Paris. Most amusingly, he had little sense of the significance of the race he had won until it was over. There was a large crowd at the finish to watch his solo victory and club officials had drunk champagne and kissed him heartily and often in the aftermath of the win and Graham had found it all a little overwhelming. I sensed from his bemusement that this was not the typical response to cycling success in Doncaster, South Yorkshire.

Such was Graham's calm re-telling of events that he gave a passable impression of having simply turned up and ridden away from the field. The way he told it made it all sound so simple and it was true that he had won on a bike that he had trained on all through the British winter. It consisted of a nice Italian frame with good, but not top of the range components. However it was certainly not the expensive range carbon-fibre model that he had been given by his sponsors in the UK and that he was expecting to use in France. A bike had been delivered, but it was the wrong size for him and he was still waiting for the replacement to arrive. Lance Armstrong's quote that it is not about the bike [but the rider] seemed highly pertinent at this point. Also, when

Graham later showed me a colour photograph taken just before he crossed the finishing line, it was clear to see that his front and back wheels were not from the same pair; a legacy of the puncture he had endured near to the end of the race.

Graham also told us that the team's level of (dis)organisation was not always to his liking. As a rule, he liked to arrive at a race at least an hour before it began and even from my limited experience of bike racing I could immediately understand why. Cycling is a sport that requires organisation and planning in order that the rider and his bike make the start line on time, fully prepared and in good working order. Stories abound of cyclists arriving at races only to find that shoes, race-kit or even the bike itself have been left at home. At this race, however, the team had arrived only 30 minutes before it had begun and this had disrupted his normal pre-race preparations and warm-up. He managed to stay calm however, by listening to music through his personal stereo and it obviously had not detracted from his performance on the day.

Despite these mitigating factors, I was still a little suspicious of Graham's casualness, knowing that in addition to raw talent it takes advanced bike-handling skills, good tactics and a strong will to win an event such as this. These things don't just happen I thought, although Graham was very impressive in painting the picture that his win just had. Beneath the easy-going veneer though, he seemed to possess a great although understated self-assuredness. It was as if he was beginning to know that he was good and expected to do well, whatever the circumstances. This was a subtle yet significant change from the young man I had met only a few weeks previously and had a clear link to his early experiences in France. Already he was growing into the role and the persona of the top-level bike rider and in this respect his demeanor was a living embodiment of the aims and ethos of the Dave Rayner Fund. One could not but be struck by how much he had taken his new life in his stride.

As we talked, Laurent returned with Sam and after our initial surprise and confusion she joined us in conversation and it became clear that the same could be said of her too. Obviously she missed Graham, but his cycling success was very much treated as a joint project. She would do anything to offer practical and emotional support and was, since meeting Graham also a cyclist herself, telling us of an impressive recent training ride of around 80 miles that she had completed with some of Graham's old training partners. Although unspoken, there was a great bond and togetherness between them that made me confident that they would endure their periods of enforced separation with a sense of joint purpose. At a simple level, it was a joy for Julia and I (who had also been together since the age of 17) to see a couple in love with each other and happy to see the other person prosper and grow.

I had told Sam that part of the reason for visiting Graham at this early stage of the season was to gain an understanding of his life off the bike in France. We had agreed therefore that we would pay a visit to the house that he was sharing with two of his team-mates. Luckily the house was only around three kilometres from the hotel and the four of us set off together to walk back through an area of out-of-town retail outlets and supermarkets. The house itself was an old bungalow style building set in a courtyard and surrounded by a development of small new houses. It had belonged to the mother of one of the team officials, but when she had passed away it was re-designated for use by the overseas members of the team. In summary, it was basic, but sound. A step down in terms of home comforts for Graham, who had previously lived with his parents in the village of Rossington outside Doncaster, but a place that offered freedom and independence and the opportunity to leave the front door open during the day. Graham had received a sizeable cup for winning Paris–Evreux and this sat on top of the sideboard in the living room. However, this was only one of the many telltale signs that the house was occupied by cyclists, as lycra clothing, various pieces of equipment and newspaper reports of the recent win were to be found on most of the available furniture and wall space.

Waiting for us were Graham's new colleagues and housemates, Caspar from Estonia and Dimitri who is Moldovan. Caspar was blond and taller and thinner than Graham and was still young enough to sport the fading signs of adolescent acne on his cheeks. Dimitri on the other hand was dark and smaller than Graham and had the build of a pure climber. Caspar as a citizen of one of the new EU countries did not need a visa to live in France, but Dimitri coming from Moldova still did. I took a photograph of the three of them together in the courtyard and as I composed the shot I was aware of just how young they all looked together and how in need of looking after they appeared to be. However, this was a mistake on my part as I was failing to acknowledge the steel in their respective characters that had brought them success to the extent that they could come together in these unusual surroundings.

Both Caspar and Dimitri were of a similar age to Graham, but both had also spent the previous season racing in France, although Caspar had lost some of the year due to having to complete his national service in the Estonian army. All three had ridden against each other in the previous year's under-23 world championship road race in Hamilton, Canada, but in addition Caspar and Dimitri had also ridden a significant number of under-23 world cup races, something which Graham had not yet done. In fact, on the surface the two were more experienced riders than Graham, but his recent success had seemed to elevate him, temporarily at least, to the top of the pecking order. When we arrived Caspar was doing what cyclists the world over do when not riding their bikes. He was cleaning his bike.

We introduced ourselves to Caspar and Dimitri, but as we discovered, things were still a little complicated language-wise between the three. Caspar spoke Estonian, Russian, English and some French, whilst Dimitri spoke Russian and French. Graham had English (obviously) and only the odd word of French and so any conversation between Graham and Dimitri had to take place through Caspar. Also, conversations between Graham and the team officials went first via Dimitri (French to Russian) and Caspar (Russian to English) and then back again. Despite this though, the three new team-mates seemed to get on well together and the state of the house, more clean and tidy than one could expect from three men in their early twenties living together, was a testament (at least when there were visitors present) to a good level of co-operation between them.

One could read many things into the domestic situation we saw, but what struck me most was that at the time, Graham, Caspar and Dimitri all needed each other in different ways. Graham seemed to be the most financially sound of the three and it was interesting to note that he thought that living in France was not overly expensive whilst both Caspar and Dimitri found the cost of living high compared to their home countries. This seemed to be confirmed when Caspar accepted Graham's half-joking offer of 3 Euros to wash his bike whilst he talked to us. It wasn't clear to me if Caspar was just being a good guy, or if he really needed the equivalent of £2 that washing the bike would bring him, but the incident brought into focus one of the key roles that the Dave Rayner Fund plays: that of simply making ends meet. Similarly, Sam had been given a long list of items by Graham to bring over on her visit, which included a particular energy drink that worked well for Graham on training rides and in competition. Caspar and Dimitri on the other hand made do with water made sweet with grenadine.

As well as their accommodation, UC Beauvais was paying the weekly shopping bill for the three and there seemed to be a vague arrangement in existence whereby they would also be given a regular allowance. However, the payment of this had to date been a little irregular and whilst this did not appear to be hurting Graham one could sense that it would make a bigger difference to the other two. On the other hand, Graham would be bound to benefit especially in the short term and as he learned the ropes, from Caspar and Dimitri's greater experience of French life and cycling.

After a friendly if halting conversation with Caspar (about of all things the weather in Estonia) and a hello to Dimitri we sat down to talk once more, this time about the bulk of the season ahead. In particular I was keen to know when Graham would be back to race in England and we discussed some of his objectives for the year. The first trip back was due to be in early April for the Archer Grand Prix, a major one-day race through the lanes of Buckinghamshire, that attracts one of the best domestic fields of the year. Graham had entered the race and was due to ride it in the colours of Doncaster Wheelers (his domestic sponsors were also the sponsors of the club) and against some of his team-mates from 2003 that were now dotted around a number of new and existing domestic set-ups. However, he had recently learned that he had been selected to ride for the Great Britain team in a three day under-23 world cup race in Belgium over the same weekend. Naturally the chance to ride in the colours of the national team would take precedence and so the Archer was now off the calendar for Graham. However, on a positive note this also meant that Graham would be back in the fold with the organisation that had decided not to select him for a full-time role in their under-23 Endurance squad.

Later in the season he hoped to return for a number of events including the Elite National road race in late June at the Celtic manor resort in South Wales and its age-group equivalent in Oxfordshire in July. Looking further ahead the chance to represent Great Britain at the World Championships in Verona in October was also a realistic prospect. I noted down the various dates and events and contemplated this half of my own exciting year on the road.

After more coffee we arranged to pick up Graham and Sam by taxi at 6.30pm for dinner in the centre of Beauvais. Graham, Caspar and Dimitri and the other under-23 riders in the team were all riding a race in Normandy on Sunday which formed part of a series known as the Maillot Jeunes and so Graham wanted to eat early in the evening. Having made the arrangement we left the four of them to watch the day's stage of the Paris–Nice race on the small portable TV in the living room of the house.

The subject of diet is one never far from the lips of top cyclists. Such is the obsession with weight (and the loss of it) in cycling that it is not unknown for top riders to succumb to eating disorders and although obviously fit, by the harsh standards of the peloton (and you must remember that these are very particular and demanding ones) Graham had weight that he could lose. However, he displayed a healthy attitude to food, neither reckless nor paranoid. Pasta formed the main part of his diet, even having it for breakfast since arriving in France. However, he could no longer get hold of baked beans (another energy giving staple), but was getting by OK without them. On the night we ate together, we struggled to find somewhere in Beauvais to have pasta and so rather than walk the streets for too long we opted instead for a Chinese meal. Graham ate sensibly throughout, sticking to rice and noodles where possible and drinking plenty of water. As with most things though, he seemed to know what he was doing and from his form to date his approach appeared to work.

Our lack of independent transport meant that we would not be able to watch Graham race on the following day, as there was insufficient room in the team cars for us to travel to Normandy. So instead we said our goodbyes on Saturday evening, promising to text or email with updates and giving our good luck wishes during the taxi ride back to our hotel. As we left Graham and Sam to make the short journey back to the team house in the taxi, we felt excited but tired after our long day. We had been impressed in so many ways with these two young people, both as a couple and also as individuals. We and many others could learn a lot from their positive attitude. At the same time, we wondered what Caspar and Dimitri's night had held for them and how they would get through the season with apparently little money. Even if they were successful and earned prize money in races as Graham had done for winning Paris–Evreux (the first prize was 300 Euros) the French Cycling Federation operates a system whereby it holds onto all prize money until the end of the season when it is distributed in lump sums to the successful riders.

On arriving back at the hotel we ordered drinks and began to relax. However, I had one last commitment to honour and one last conversation to conduct that day. I had promised Cheeky Phil that I would ring him whilst we were in France and I had attempted to contact him once or twice during the day, but had been met be the sound of a voice message in French, but spoken in a Chadderton (half Oldham and half Manchester) accent informing me that he wasn't available and that I should leave a message. However, on this occasion I did get through, and Phil told me that he had been at work all day at Decathlon sports in Avranche and had been unable to answer the phone. He immediately began to enthuse about Graham's result. Phil knew the town of Evreux well, having lived there during his first year in France (coincidence striking again) and according to him winning Paris–Evreux is a massive step towards gaining a professional contract. In fact, Graham's achievement was only overshadowed by the win of Jamie Alberts, another of the 2004 crop, in an even bigger race in southern France on the same day. My thoughts went back at this point to my conversation with the Committee at the 2004 selection meeting when they had stressed the need for someone from the next crop of riders to make the breakthrough to the top level of the professional ranks, and as Phil told me about the significance of Graham's win and also that of Jamie Alberts, I wondered if either or both of these two young riders would be the source of the longed-for next wave of success.

Phil was also keen to learn about Graham's domestic situation and to pass on one or two tips about life with housemates (especially those from poorer countries) and it struck me what a selfless fellow he is. His own season was now under way, but he was more than happy to talk up the success of another bike rider and to share his own early experiences with us. Phil himself had only raced once to date in 2004 (the first race fell victim to snow) and was going through a period of adjustment, now having to arrange his training around work, something which he had not had to do in previous years. However, as we talked with the sound of Phil's adoptive French family having dinner in the background, there was little doubt that he was happy and content with the choices he had made.

Sitting in the bar of the hotel in Beauvais I was aware that cycling had offered a pathway to a different and fulfilling life for a whole host of people from various parts of the world, whether they were from Chadderton and Doncaster or Estonia and Moldova. I also mused on the unintended consequences of the work of the Dave Rayner Fund. Phil Evans had a life in France in which cycling was now only a part. His girlfriend was French and this was the place that he now called home. Of course cycling was still very important, but it was not the whole reason for him being there. However, without his talent on a bike and the Dave Rayner Fund's mission to nurture that talent, he would probably never have even glimpsed the life that he now regarded as his norm.

At one point in our conversation Phil described to me the profile of the small final circuit on which Graham had won Paris–Evreaux and likened a steep climb near the finish to a particular hill that he knows in Milnrow near Rochdale. It's near Dave Grogan's house he said, referring to one of the more colourful characters from his days with ABC Centreville. This made me smile; I'm not sure why, but it just did, and I was still smiling when I awoke on the following day.

CHAPTER 5

A Day in the Life

ON RETURNING FROM France, I now wanted to make contact with Tom. At our first meeting, he had given me the number on which he could be contacted in Belgium, so in a quiet moment in the working day I made a call, to find out how he had been faring since arriving in the country and to pencil in a date for my second trip of the year.

The phone was answered and I asked if the voice on the other end was Tom. 'No, it's Roger,' came the reply. This was Roger Hammond, the 2003 British Road Race Champion who I knew was to be Tom's landlord for the season. Roger is a talented and experienced professional who in the early stages of his career was the World Junior Cyclo-Cross champion and who now rode for the Belgian MrBookmaker.com team. Roger has carved out a fine career for himself on the continent and this was likely to be a productive environment in which for Tom to live. In the first two years of his stay in Belgium he had resided in the team house, on the outskirts of Brussels. However, coming after three years of student life, Tom had finally outgrown this communal mode of living, so in his third year he had lived on his own (house sitting for an ex-pat Briton). Although having many advantages this had proved ultimately to be too solitary, but now Tom seemed to have found a balance, living with a top-level professional as well as another young British cyclist, Matt Brindle (a friend from Tom's university days). Tom had the company of two other bike riders, but was free from the demands of living with a large group of relative strangers from another country.

Roger handed the phone to Tom and we began to discuss events since we had last met. Following our meeting at his parents' house he had left for Spain and a few weeks working on a training camp. Tom's employer was Graham Baxter (another committee member of the Fund) and the deal for Tom was a good one, in that he had an expenses-paid trip away to train and in return was asked to lead one of the daily rides undertaken by the paying guests on the camp. Sometimes, however, this was not as simple as it sounds, in that he was something of a target for one or two of the keener and more talented amateurs who were on the camp. On some days therefore the riding was a little harder and more competitive than he would have preferred at that time of the year. Professional pride though meant that he found it difficult to simply let his would-be challengers have their day, however determined they were to claim a professional scalp.

The phenomenon of the winter racer is well known in cycling. These are riders who give their biggest efforts on what are supposedly easy training runs and who get maximum pleasure from hurting colleagues and team-mates when they are in the process of building their own fitness. Once the spring comes around and the true racing season begins they tend to disappear. Seldom do they take part in a real race. It was in some ways reassuring for me to realise that Tom too suffers at the hands of these creatures.

Following the training camps, which had done much to bring on Tom's form, he had headed to Belgium. His method of transport from home was a cross-channel car ferry, as this allowed him to transport 'the silver bird', his automotive pride and joy, with him. Tom's car is a huge old silver Mercedes saloon. Although in real terms it not worth thousands, it is still something of a classic and no doubt it must turn heads when driven around Yorkshire during the winter months.

Once in Belgium, the season had begun well and he had gained a 9th place in the first race of the season, the Molenbeek–

Wersbeek Kermesse. A Kermesse is a singularly Belgian type of event. Usually based around a town centre, the race will usually involve multiple laps of a relatively short course with an emphasis on the crowd seeing the riders at regular intervals. These make up the staple diet of Belgian cycling and once the season is in full swing there is barely a day that goes by without a Kermesse taking place somewhere in the country. In addition to Tom's good performance, the race had been won by one of his Australian teammates, Phil Thuaux, which was good for spirits all round.

After my warm experiences in Beauvais, I was keen to arrange a visit to see Tom in person. This time though I wanted to take in a race. Tom consulted his calendar and we discussed events that I could come over for. In the end we decided on a visit in the week after Easter and that I would come with him to a major one-day race in Holland called Veenendaal–Veenendaal. This would be one of the biggest races that the team would take part in during the season and the majority of the other riders taking part would be from division one or two teams. Up to the 2004 season, professional cycling teams were organised into divisions based on how successful they were. The teams that take part in the Tour de France were for the most part from division one, whilst Tom's team was from the lowest rung of the professional ladder, division three. However, it is sometimes possible for teams from different divisions to take part in the same races, but this is dependant on the team receiving an invitation from the organisers of the race. Compared to the big trade teams the budget of Cyclingnews.com is small. However, thanks to the efforts of its management and riders, it has come a long way quickly and one wouldn't bet against them rising up further through the professional ranks. The consciously Australian image and identity of the team has been a key element in the marketing of the team. Many event organisers are keen to invite the team to add the spice of something different to their races and this was the case with Veenendaal–Veenendaal, which was due to take place on Friday 16th April.

After agreeing to talk again soon, we ended our conversation and I began to look into my travel arrangements for the visit. In the end I decided that my best course was to travel to London on Wednesday and to stay with my brother, who had recently moved to Camden. Then on Thursday, I would fly from Heathrow to Brussels. Tom would meet me at the airport and we would go for a coffee or a meal to catch up and to set the agenda for the following day's race. Friday would be taken up with the race itself and then I would fly back on Saturday for a weekend in London where I would be joined by Julia. It all sounded great, but as with all the best-laid plans it was ultimately due to be thrown out of the window.

It was the afternoon of Good Friday when my mobile phone went. I was sat at home and it was Tom on the line. He had just been told that the team was no longer taking part in Veenendaal–Veenendaal and my plans had just gone up in smoke. Instead the team was taking part in a significant race in Northern France, the Grand Prix de Denain. This formed part of the prestigious Coup de France series and would again contain a number of division one teams. The only problem was that the race was on Thursday 15th April, the day I was due to travel to Belgium. Tom said that I was still welcome to come, but obviously I needed to re-jig my travel arrangements, and fast. He was very apologetic for the last minute change, but said that this was very much part of the pro-cyclist's life. As we talked I was aware that professional sport is probably not a good career choice for those who like order and predictability in their lives. Before he rang off Tom also said that he would try to arrange for me to ride in the team car during the race, if I could in fact get there.

I spent the following hours on the internet and telephone attempting to re-book my flights and discussing different travel options with Tom, who was sat in Roger's living room in Belgium. It was a tense time in the house as Roger was due to ride Paris–Roubaix on Easter Sunday. This is perhaps the best known and to many people the most punishing of the early season Spring one-day classics. Well over one hundred miles in length, the race takes in numerous cobbled sections of road, known as Pavé. In some ways it is more about survival than racing and every year the majority of the field do not even make it to the finish in the open air velodrome in Roubaix in Northern France. As if to emphasise the gruesome nature of the race, it is colloquially known as the Hell of the North and to rub the suffering in a wee bit more the winner's trophy consists of a single cobble-stone. I had been keen from day one that this would not be another book about the suffering of cyclists, but stories such as this show what a temptation it is to go down this road.

Eventually I finalised my new arrangements. My original flights were non-changeable, so I had to cancel them. Luckily I was able to book an alternative flight for only £40 using one of the no-frills airlines. I would now drive down to Stansted on Wednesday and fly directly to Charleroi. Thursday would be Denain and I would come back to England on Friday. The only downside of the plan was the time of the return flight: 6.40am.

I could now relax a little and I embarked on a short Easter tour of Lancashire and the Yorkshire dales with two long-standing friends. One the first day we did some 96 miles before reaching our overnight stop in Kirkby Lonsdale, which sits on the boundary of Lancashire, the Lake District and the Dales, where we were joined by our respective wives and partners. On day two and hindered by the effects of a good night down the pub we decided on a more modest route to Settle via some of the most picturesque roads in the Dales. Easter Sunday dawned overcast and we lingered over a full English breakfast and the Sunday papers before setting off. However, by the time we reached the hills above Ingleton the skies had cleared and we were treated to a sunlit vision of the wonderful Victorian rail viaduct at Ribblehead. By mid-afternoon we were back at the starting point of the tour, the village of Waddington, just north of Clitheroe. The bikes were loaded into our cars and we set off for home. For me the shortened second day had a second major compensation: I could watch Paris–Roubaix at home on television. Obviously I would be keen to see how Roger was getting on and when I switched on the TV I was excited to find that he was towards the front of the field, although the race was still in its early stages. My excitement levels rose still further as the leading group was whittled down to six towards the end and Roger was still there.

The weather plays a great part in the race as if it rains, the cobble-stones become even more treacherous. In fact there are many evocative photographs of riders and bikes completely covered in mud at the end of the race. Today, though, it was clear, but more importantly it was dry. I was on the edge of my seat, but then the effects of my own exertions (and the previous night's drink) began to take hold and I felt myself begin to slide into sleep. I fought it, but it was to no avail. When I awoke some fifteen minutes later the group was down to four and to my delight there was Roger; resplendent in his British Champion's jersey. The group entered the velodrome and my level of anticipation went up a couple more notches. No British rider had ever won this race; the best was a third place by Barry Hoban, but this had been some years before. If Roger won it would change his life. In fact as long as he didn't fall off in the next two minutes his life would change anyway. The four men positioned themselves for the final sprint and then in a blur it was over. Had Roger won?

The answer was no. The winner, by inches, was the Swedish rider and sometime resident of South Wales, Magnus Backstedt. Roger had been placed third, equalling Barry Hoban's performance, but this was a massively significant result. Roger's career and profile had just taken a major step up and he would instantly become a man in demand. Again events had set my forthcoming trip in a fortuitous context, even though this time it was in a more indirect way.

I set off on my long drive south on Wednesday, eager to see for myself how Tom's year was progressing, but also keen to see how his landlord's success had changed things around the house. My drive was thankfully uneventful and I checked in on time and went through to the departure lounge where I bought a newspaper and sat down to each lunch. As usual I began to read the paper from the back pages and tucked inside was a very small article which changed my mood completely. The story was of a British rider based in France who was reported to have failed a drugs test. The rider had won a number of early season races in the south of the country and had been tested following one of these victories. The test had revealed traces of a steroid. He had been stripped of his wins and reportedly sacked by his club. Worst of all, the rider was one of those supported by the Fund. It felt like a punch in the stomach. Was all my belief and optimism misplaced? Was I naïve to want to tell a positive story?

It sometimes feels that the only cycling story one ever reads in the national press concerns doping, but amongst the paranoia and feeling of being oppressed there are still the facts (or at least the apparent facts) to consider. The rider did not deny taking the substance, but questioned whether it was in fact illegal. Now I was eager, but for different reasons. I wanted (and almost felt obliged) to glean Tom's attitude to banned substances.

The flight to Belgium was short and I emerged from Charleroi airport to find him parking up the Silver Bird. My first impression was of someone who was seriously enjoying life. He had acquired something of a sun-tan since our winter meeting, together with a single streak of blonde through his brown spiky hair. I climbed into the car and we set off on the 40-minute drive around the main Brussels ring road to Terverun where I was due to stay for two nights. My first questions were about the state of his form and the news was good on this front. He too had enjoyed success since we last talked and had gained a third place in another race in Belgium. This was his first podium placing during his season in the country and this had unsurprisingly put him in a positive frame of mind.

Then I hesitantly raised the subject of the news of the British rider's failed drugs test. Part of me was unsure about the probity of this. I was still clear that my purpose was not to write an exposé, but at the same time it was something that would be bound to cause a ripple throughout the sport in Britain. Tom's response was honest and frank and did much to help me understand more about drugs in sport. To sum up our conversation, Tom's view was that everyone in cycling (and other sports for that matter) has a personal choice to make. At the same time there is a massive grey area around what is and what is not legal and acceptable. The list of banned substances, far from being fixed, for example, actually changes at regular intervals. As a result, even the honest sportsman can fail a test, although ignorance is not accepted as a reasonable defence.

This prompted me to think more deeply on the subject and on reflection I realised that we, as members of the public, are often offered the issue of drugs in sport in overtly simplistic terms. Also, it is served up to us drenched in a moralism which owes much to the heritage of the Victorians and their view of the purpose of sport in society. In my younger days I had studied the history of sport in some depth and so know the origins of much of our thinking about its worth, purpose and values. The Victorians did much to codify the rules of modern sports and this was almost always done in the light of something called the 'amateur ethos'. Think fair play and the gentleman sportsman and you are on the right lines. The problem though is that this was and is a fallacy. Rules have always been bent and broken even by those that we now see as embodiments of the noble values of sport. The famous cricketer, W.G. Grace for example, was not above ignoring the fact that he had been given out and simply carrying on with his innings. What I am trying to say here is that we are hampered in our view of cheating in sport by a belief that it is somehow different from other endeavours. Put simply it is not. Instead it is subject to all the ambiguity and double standards of the rest of our lives.

In addition, such is the complexity of the issue that a substance can be legal one day and not the next. Also, the dividing line between legal supplements and illegal drugs can be a blurred and subjective one and as both are sometimes manufactured in the same factories, it is not surprising that things can get mixed up (on both physical and philosophical levels). Another element to the debate is linked to the level of performance expected by the audience. We as spectators demand excellence at all time, without paying any heed to the physical toll that this takes on athletes. On the negative side, cycling has acquired a particularly poor reputation regarding drugs. However, as with all illicit activity, the only time we find out about it is when someone gets caught. Who is to say then, that other sports are not just better at covering up their misdemeanours? It is fair to say, for example, that few professional footballers have failed a blood test for EPO. However, how many people know that many national governing bodies don't actually even test for it?

I felt better informed having spoken to Tom. It isn't that cycling is inherently 'clean', but equally it is not a lost cause and we are wrong if we think that every good performance is done on the back of doping. It's all too easy to be seduced by sensationalist stories of 'drug cheats' in sport and to cast down our uninformed value judgements on people and circumstances that we don't really know. However, in the end these are simply individuals who sometimes make a genuine mistake or who are sometimes tempted just like the rest of us. The major differences though are twofold. The first is the strength of the spotlight that is thrown on them if their weakness is discovered and the second is the potential effect on their health if they make a certain choice. In the absolute worst case, the wrong decision can even lead to death.

After examining my own prejudices and consequently re-positioning my thoughts, I was happy to move on to lighter matters and having checked into my hotel we decided to go out for pizza. We talked about many things during our meal, but one of the main subjects was the aftermath of Roger's success in Roubaix. Basically things had gone mad. Roger had been inundated with requests for interviews and had even appeared on Belgian TV in what I think Tom described as the equivalent of the Des O'Connor show. My mind spun at the prospect of a Belgian Des O'Connor, but whatever the quality of the programme, it was all the result of the third place and showed how important cycling is in Belgium. It was a wave to be ridden and it appeared that Roger was doing this. Tom told me that he had been given the day off by the team management from the next day's race and was going instead to spend it at the Zolder Grand Prix circuit, where he would be racing classic cars, as a present from one of the team's main sponsors. So while Tom and company would be riding through the roads of one of the more drab parts of Northern France, Roger would be enjoying a day of more speed and considerably less effort.

We made our arrangements for the following day over dinner.

I would be picked up in the morning from the hotel and we would travel to the race with another British professional from the MrBookmaker.com team (and twice British Road Race Champion) Jeremy Hunt, together with one of Tom's Aussie team-mates Hilton Clarke. Tom dropped me back at the hotel and after making a call home I sat down to enjoy the remainder of my evening.

Thursday dawned warm and sunny and Jeremy's red Volvo estate pulled up outside the hotel dead on time. I got in and Tom introduced me to Jeremy (Jez) and Hilton. There was a sense of nervous excitement in the car as we set off at high speed south towards the French border. This was further fuelled by Jez's driving which was to say the least aggressive. But here were three young men off to race bikes for a living and contrary to the image that many in the UK have of cycling, to have a highly-charged experience. Indeed, competitive cycling, particularly road racing, creates a buzz more akin to extreme sports than to a sedate pastime. They were living the life and who could blame them.

At first the three talked mainly amongst themselves, which I understood and accepted, about the race to come and about some of their colleagues and adversaries. Of course much of this was gossip, but who doesn't gossip about their workmates? Then Jez asked me where I was from and inadvertently set off another of those 'it's a small world' stories which came to characterise my experiences. I replied that I lived north of Bury and he told me that he had been born and brought up in a small village some two miles from where I now called home. Jez's southern English accent gave no hint of this, but it transpired that he had moved to Devon when he was in his teens. In another scarcely believable twist I was later to be told by a friend at Centreville that Jez was for a time actually a member of our club before departing for the South-West with the family and that he had ridden the club's evening timetrial on a number of occasions in the company of – guess who? – Phil Evans. I was by this point increasingly convinced that all roads led back to Cheeky Phil. However, the rule of six degrees of separation was in my view overly complex, as I was usually able to get back to him in only one or two leaps.

Our shared experiences of Ramsbottom and Summerseat (the village in which Jez had grown up) served as something of an ice-breaker and the remainder of the drive was much more relaxed, despite his driving. He had recently bought the car and was keen to see what it could do on the open road and it was duly noted that the heady atmosphere here would be in stark contrast to the tension evident in the various team buses and cars that were also heading to the race. In no time we passed the border into France and shortly after we arrived at the race headquarters. This was a school in a nearby town to Denain. The remainder of the Cyclingnews.com team had already arrived and I was introduced to the four other guys that were riding that day and to Gilbert, the team manager. Tom had succeeded in getting me a ride in the team car for the day and I was also introduced to Daniel who would be driving. Daniel, I later found out, was in fact Danny Willems, a well-known ex-pro who had been something of a star in his day. In fact at one point early in his career he had been given that eternal kiss of death that is the label, 'the next Eddy Merckx'. I sat in the school gymnasium that was being used as the HQ for the race and watched as the team went through the pre-race ritual of pinning their numbers to the shirts, getting changed and then receiving a final leg massage from the team soigneur. Outside the team mechanic was making his final preparations to the bikes. After a brief talk from Gilbert the six Cyclingnews.com riders emerged and got on their carbon-fibre Ridley machines and made their way across to the town square where they would sign on and be presented to the healthy crowd that had assembled to see the race depart.

One of the great things about cycling is the accessibility of its stars to the public and many of the one hundred plus riders that were taking part that day were simply standing around in the square with the spectators. Some were taking the opportunity to catch up with friends that rode for other teams and others were simply collecting their thoughts. The field for the day included Bradley McGee and the thought crossed my mind to seek him out and to introduce myself to him, saying, 'You don't know me but I met your Mum and Dad once.' In the end though, I decided against this and turned instead to talk to one or two of Tom's team-mates. One of these was Matt Rice, who I found out was originally from Tasmania and who was in his second spell as a full-time bike-rider. Once before he had given the game away and gone back home to a full-time job, only to find that he missed the excitement of bike racing. In mid-conversation, Matt simply stopped talking and I wondered what I had done to antagonise him. Then I realised that he was simply posing whilst a fan took his photograph. This I found, together with signing autographs, was all part and parcel of the role. In fact, some of the autograph hunters had specially printed sheets and would ask the rider to sign in maybe two or three boxes. This would allow them to easily trade riders' signatures with other enthusiasts.

I remembered at this point that I was supposed to be in the team car, but for the life of me I couldn't find it. There were so many people and vehicles in the square that I simply could not locate my ride. Luckily Gilbert was in control of the situation and he managed to find me and to guide me to the car, just before the flag went up for the race to start. I was directed to the front passenger seat and buckled on my seatbelt just as the field began to head out of town. Team cars are allotted numbers and for the most part they must remain in sequence during the race. The exceptions to this are if a rider suffers a puncture or mechanical problem, in which case the car can drop back, or the team has a rider in a break at the head of the field, in which case it can move up.

However, the first few miles of a race are what is known as neutralised. This allows the field to head out at a relatively easy pace and in formation, before they effectively hit a second start line and begin racing for real. One of the purposes of the neutralised zone is to allow the riders to correct any mechanical problems that they may discover and to answer the call of nature and I was surprised to see a succession of riders standing by the road in the first few miles relieving themselves of unwanted liquid ballast (or taking a piss).

Then the race began proper and almost immediately a break went away. We knew this through the official race radio that was giving reports to all the team cars. Unfortunately for me, the broadcast was in French and so I had only a limited understanding of what was going on. In fact as the race unfolded I realised that the team car, although necessary to support the riders, is not the best place from which to watch a race. In fact one of my lasting memories of the day is of periods of simply staring at the back of the black car in front that belonged to the MBK Oktos team. For long interludes nothing happened and I even managed to fall asleep for a few minutes. Not intentionally, of course, and I hoped that my sunglasses hid the fact from my fellow travellers. All hell could be breaking loose up the road, but we were in a largely silent bubble. In fact, the driver and mechanic seldom spoke to each other let alone to me and this added to the surrealism of the experience. Occasionally Daniel would communicate with the team's riders via another radio, but for minutes on end there was little actual activity in the car.

Things heated up for a while when Hilton suffered a mechanical problem which forced him to the back of the group. The mechanic had to replace his back wheel, but such was the rush that the wheel was not fitted properly and after riding a few hundred yards Hilton had to dismount and put the new wheel in himself. There then unfolded a few minutes of pure adrenalin rush as Hilton attempted to get back into the main group using the team car as an impromptu windbreak. This, together with getting a physical pull from a car, is strictly illegal as well as dangerous, but the authorities tend to turn a blind eye to it. Flying along at around forty miles per hour whilst holding on to a car is not good for the nerves, but shows the bravery (or foolhardiness depending on your point of view) that forms an often overlooked element of cycling. Our car slalomed up the road through the other race vehicles with Hilton in tow. Eventually he made it back to the group and the car fell silent again, but this time more than usual. My mind strayed to the common scene in Westerns when one of the characters would say, 'it's quiet, too quiet'. I looked at Daniel and Daniel looked at the mechanic and then we all looked at the radio. It was broken. Now we had no idea how things were unfolding up the road and if any of the Cyclingnews.com team were in the leading group. Luckily by now the race had reached the point where it was doing a series of laps of a fairly small finishing circuit around Denain. As part of this, Gilbert and all the other team managers and soigneurs were located by the side of the road at a designated feed station. The next time around we screeched to a halt and an instruction for a new radio was quickly made and answered.

The race was now over three hours old and a number of riders had already 'packed' for the day and were heading for the showers. I had no idea if Tom was one of these, but hoped that he was hanging in somewhere. Successfully connected up to race radio again, we realised that one of the team members, Cameron Jennings, was in a group up the road. It was not the actual leading group, but it did mean that the race officials would allow us to navigate our way around the main field and to drive up the road to them. Daniel duly put his foot down and we were soon doing around seventy along a narrow road. Again a long period of inactivity had ended with a burst of extreme speed. We spent the remainder of the race positioned behind a small group of around eight riders and I was in awe of the speed that they managed to maintain as the race neared the end of its fourth hour. Finally the group set up for its final sprint up the home straight and the car was directed off the road and towards an area where all the teams would re-convene at the end of the race. We pulled up in the car park of a civic sports centre still not knowing who had won and how Tom had fared.

Hilton was already there, having pulled out after further mechanical problems, but it was clear from his demeanour that he wasn't yet ready to talk. Eventually Tom returned with some of his team-mates, looking as one would after riding you bike at over 25 mph for four hours. There was now a steady stream of riders heading to and from the sports centre where they were able to shower and to get changed. Some of the fans from earlier in the day were also there, taking photographs and asking for autographs. I thought how different the 'after' shots must have looked to the 'before' pictures taken in the town square some hours ago. Also, there was now a roaring trade going on in appropriating whatever memorabilia was available from the race. The plastic race numbers that are attached to the riders' bikes were particularly popular with the throng, as were the bidons (the water bottles) that the riders drink from.

One of the things that struck me at the end of the race was the lack of ceremony or fuss. After changing, most of the riders had only a few minutes to reflect on the day before they were ushered into their transport to set off back to the various parts of France or Belgium from where they had come. That was it. Ride yourself into the ground for hours, get clean and go home. I thanked Gilbert for the day and we began to look for Jez. Luckily he had arranged a ride for us back to his car and we soon set off heading north. The three riders began to reflect on the race and I listened in, all the time feeling a total fraud, having spent my afternoon in a car (and having fallen asleep) whilst they had been digging deep into their physical and psychological resources.

The race had been won by the Norwegian rider Thor Hushovdt, from the Irishman Mark Scanlon. Tom had missed the first break (whilst answering a call of nature) and had spent the rest of the day trying to get on terms again. It occurred to me at this point how much road racing is a game of chance and how there are many circumstances in which the strongest rider will not win, or not be allowed to win. He had, however, competed strongly during the race and had at one point ridden across from one group to another. This may not sound overly impressive to the uninitiated, but it takes a great deal of strength to establish and maintain a speed which is greater than that of a group of riders. In addition, riding alone or at the front of a group exposes a rider to the effects of the wind, whereas those behind can tuck in and maintain the same speed with considerably less effort. All in all Tom's ride was a quality one in a high quality race. It may not have made the headlines, but he could still feel proud with his efforts on the day.

Heading towards the Belgian border, the journey was interrupted by the sound of a mobile phone. It was Roger ringing Tom to find out how the day had gone and to bring news of his own trip to Zolder. The contrast between the two afternoons could not really have been wider. Roger's day had been characterised by fast cars and beautiful women, whilst the other three had been working hard on their bikes on the roads of northern France. Not that anyone begrudged Roger his day. Everyone knew that it had been earned with his great efforts in Paris–Roubaix, but also in a number of other early season classic races in which he had also done well.

It was agreed that the three would meet up with Roger and Matt (who had also spent the day racing cars) at the same Pizzeria that Tom and I had eaten at the night before. To my surprise and joy the invitation was extended to me. This was a generous touch on their part as they could easily have dropped me back at the hotel before they went out. So it was we strolled up the quiet main street of Terverun towards the eaterie. Stood at the back of the group I could see the toll that the race had taken by the way the three were walking. Such was the state of their legs that it was like watching three sore cowboys moseying on into town.

What followed was the simple sight of friends having a good time together. Everyone was in good form with no-one safe from the humour of the others. They even got stuck into me at one point, but in a strange way felt it like a privilege and I was happy just to be there drinking in the atmosphere. Later Tom was at pains to point out that it wasn't always as good as this and I understood his point. There would be plenty of times during a season when the weather is bad, when the going is hard and when the rewards seem far away. However, when I looked around the table that night I saw five men who shared the collective sense of simply having the best job in the world.

I awoke at 4am on the following day in order to make my way to the airport for my early flight home. I was back in England by 8am and as I ate breakfast in the terminal at Stansted airport, before driving into London I marvelled at how fortunate I had been to enjoy my very own day in the life.

CHAPTER 6

A Slight Return

AFTER THE HIGHS of my April trip to Belgium I had to return, for a few weeks at least, to the more mundane world of work. I was following Graham and Tom only on a part-time basis. Having to earn a living whilst pursuing my own dream meant that I had to come to terms with having short but regular interludes of non-activity between my adventures. However, May brought Tom back to the UK on two occasions ensuring that the journey would soon begin again. His first visit was over the weekend of the 8th and 9th when he rode as part of a Cyclingnews.com team in the Lincoln Grand Prix. The Lincoln is 102 miles in length and one of the most prestigious road races in the UK. In fact it arguably ranks only second to the British Road Race Championships in terms of importance and profile. The main supporter of the race is the Lincoln City Council, but it also receives extensive help from local businesses and many of the cycling clubs in the area.

In many ways the event shows the way forward for bike racing in this country. The Council has the great advantage of an historic and dramatic town centre to offer as a backdrop for the race, and it does everything to ensure that it is shown off to its best possible effect. The race therefore acts as an opportunity to market Lincoln to prospective visitors and to showcase the city. It is in some ways surprising that more local authorities have not latched onto the idea. The likes of York, Edinburgh, Chester,

Durham and Canterbury, with their historic centres, spring to mind as ideal backdrops for top quality bike races. In addition, cities such as Birmingham, Leeds and Manchester could also use cycle races to display their urban regeneration to the wider world. Part of the promotion of the race lies in inviting teams from the continent and Cyclingnews.com had been asked to take part in the race for the second time in three years. Its appearance was as one of the strongest teams and this was in stark contrast to the Grand Prix de Denain in which it was in effect fighting above its weight.

Such has been the lack of status and perhaps more importantly, the lack of money in road racing in the UK over the last decade that it is rare to attract teams from outside the country to compete. However, the Lincoln manages to do this and in addition to Cyclingnews.com there were also teams from France and Holland taking part. It was hoped that the national teams of Uganda and Kyrgyzstan would also be involved to further broaden the appeal of the race, but at the last minute they had fallen foul of the Home Office and had been refused visas (which must have been something of a mixed blessing to the race announcers). At one point it looked as though Graham would also be taking part either in the colours of Doncaster Wheelers or in those of the Great Britain under-23 team. However, a typically late change of racing plans meant that he was instead racing in France for UC Beauvais Oise over this particular weekend.

I spoke to Tom on the telephone in the week leading up to the race and found that this was going to be something of a smash and grab raid. A group of six Cyclingnews.com riders including Tom and fellow Brit Hamish Haynes would travel over by ferry to Dover on the Saturday before the race before driving north and staying in a hotel on the outskirts of Lincoln. Sunday morning would be taken up with a quick reconnaissance of the course and the race itself would start at 11.30am. Immediately following the four hours plus of the race, they would make their return journey to Belgium and would get home some time in the early hours of Monday morning. Initially, Tom's sparring partner Hilton Clarke had been selected to ride in the race, but a bad crash had left him with that most typical of cyclist's injuries, a broken collar-bone. He was now unable to compete and had in fact been in hospital in the week leading up to the race having had an operation to help speed up his recovery. Tom's hectic schedule served to exemplify another central part of the professional cyclist's life: that of living out of a suitcase. There may be plenty of travel associated with the job, but this should not be confused with glamour. In most instances riders must have very little sense of the place they are in and it is the quality of the roads rather than the buildings and people that often makes a more lasting impression. Perhaps the most well known piece of highway on the route of the Lincoln is Michaelgate, a steep 1 in 6 cobbled street that climbs from the centre of Lincoln up to the castle and cathedral. Michaelgate is climbed some 13 times during the race and as a result, the spectators are ensured a regular close-up view of the riders working hard, but at a much slower pace than normal, to get up the hill.

I left home at 9.30am on the morning of the race and drove over to Lincoln alone. At first the crowd was fairly sparse and I was somewhat disappointed. By this time, I was developing an almost evangelical zeal for the sport and I could not understand why more people did not share this. As I stood by the finishing line at the top of Michaelgate, part of me wanted to run back into the middle of town to round up all the people who were window shopping or were sitting in coffee house, to tell them that there was a bike race going on and that they might actually enjoy it. However, I didn't need to do this. What I had forgotten was that the race was again in its early stages. The crowd would surely grow over the course of the day and true enough it had reached a highly respectable size by the last part of the race.

An early crash took care of the previous year's winner Mark Lovatt. I had arranged to meet two friends at the race and when Lovatt pottered past the finishing line for a final time before 'packing' one of them exclaimed, 'Look, it's that helpful man from our local bike shop!' This was in fact the case, as Mark works for part of the week in a shop in Macclesfield, again telling us much about our domestic cycling heroes. They are so accessible and the sport so unpretentious that the elites and the enthusiasts regularly come together. In fact, I had also seen this top British rider only the day before, where he was supporting his wife Karen, as she was taking part in a time trial on the lanes of Cheshire. I was later able to brag to friends about beating Mark Lovatt ...'s wife over 25 miles.

As the race developed, the three of us decided to move over to Michaelgate and the events that took place there gave us another insight into the tactics and politics of a road race. When the riders moved onto the climb they almost all headed for the gutters of the street, as they offered a smoother surface than the cobbled centre of the road. This brought them up close to the crowd, but still did not guarantee a straightforward ride up the hill. At one point an obviously tired rider managed to pull his shoe from his pedal. He quickly came to a dead stop and was further rewarded for his endeavours by being called a 'fucking idiot' by his immediate pursuer. At this point the three of us froze, not knowing how, or even if we were allowed, to help. After a very pregnant pause the rider managed to get his foot back in and a more confident member of the crowd ran some twenty yards down the hill to give him a push, to provide some momentum for the remainder of the climb. Again this is not strictly legal, but at the same time it is not uncommon either and it is noticeable how often the sport can involve a degree of audience participation, either intentional or unwitting. Also, the intervention of the crowd is not always welcomed by the participants, and there are well-known cases of spectators actually causing crashes, with over-enthusiastic amateur photographers who lean over barriers or who stand in the road often to blame. Events such as the one on Michaelgate also show that the budding road racer has to learn to take care of himself very quickly. There is much kidology and abuse to be suffered in the peloton and it is not a sport for the shy and retiring. Anyone who steps out of line and breaches the unwritten rules of the pack is likely to find himself on the end of a verbal tirade, or worse, very soon afterwards.

After a gradual process of whittling down, a small group of riders was left in front and two men made it together onto

Michaelgate for the final time. These were the Irishman David O'Loughlin of the Total Cycling team and British rider Robin Sharman from Recycling.co.uk. Over the course of the climb O'Loughlin managed to shrug off Sharman's challenge and he emerged alone at the top to win by ten seconds. Top rider for the Cyclingnews.com team was Cody Stevenson who was eighth. Well over half of the starters did not finish the race, but Tom crossed the line in the main body of the field. Again he had done a strong ride, but maybe without the fireworks necessary to attract the attention of press and potential sponsors.

Just before the end of the race the heavens had opened and the riders and crowd received a drenching. I said my goodbyes to my friends and set off to prepare to catch up with Tom after he crossed the finishing line. Standing there in the rain as the riders came in, I was reminded of his statement that not all days were as good as Denain and today had indeed offered the stark contrast that he had spoken of. Despite the good organisation and the large crowd, this had been one hard day with the rain acting as a cherry on the cake. For most of the field Lincoln had been all about graft and at one point a rider came to a halt beside me as I leant on a crush barrier. He looked totally drained and it was taking all his remaining strength to simply keep himself upright. I offered to help him with his bike, but he shook his head to say he was OK. It was as if he was too tired even to speak. Some seconds later Tom came past, also looking understandably fatigued, but thankfully he was able to respond to my greeting. Due to the weather, though, he was reluctant to stop and talk and instead he mouthed that I should meet him back at the race HQ, a local leisure centre. I nodded and began to run after him up the road, but with no real idea where I was going. He was soon out of sight and I became part of a drawn-out line of people who were all making their way back there.

Eventually I reached the car park to see a succession of reunions taking place between riders and their loved ones. I noticed that Tom's parents, as well as his girlfriend, Liv, and his brother were standing in the entrance to the building sheltering from the rain. I considered going over to say hello, but something stopped me. For some reason I felt that this was not the right time to intervene. Instead, I decided to simply observe from a distance and the events that followed proved this to be the best course of action. After some minutes, Tom emerged from a side door and made his way back to one of the team cars, where he was met by the family that he had not seen for some months. However, he was only able to have the briefest of hugs and conversations with his family before being ushered into one of the team cars. And then they were gone. The team was heading to Dover and the Barras family were on their way back to Keighley. It was a poignant and melancholy moment and I was glad not to have intruded upon it.

I began to walk back through the heavy rain towards the centre of Lincoln. The post race clear-up operation was now in full flow. Roads were now open to traffic again and the crush barriers were being removed from around the finishing line. There would soon be no trace that a major bike race had taken place here. I drove home in more rain that evening, clear that I had seen the other side of the coin that Tom had warned me about. Stopping off at a service station I gave Tom a ring on his mobile to ask him for his thoughts on the race. By this time, the two team cars were speeding south for the ferry ride back to mainland Europe and even down the phone it was clear that the mood in Tom's vehicle was subdued and this was hardly surprising, given the whistle-stop nature of the trip.

Tom's second springtime journey back to the UK was a thankfully less frenetic affair and one that would allow him to spend some time with his family. The reason for the trip was to compete in the British National Criterium Championships on Sunday 23rd May. A Criterium (or Crit as it is commonly known) takes place over a number of laps of a short, often town-centre-based circuit. This year the event was being held over 80 kilometres of the Hillingdon Cycle Circuit – a dedicated venue located in a fairly anonymous part of the western outskirts of the capital. Again we spoke in the week leading up to the event. I arranged to meet him at the event again, but this time he would be riding alone and not as part of the team and this meant that he should have more control of his time either side of the event.

Tom flew back from Belgium on Friday and travelled south

with Mum, Dad and brother on the morning of the race. This was going to be a big day for Tom as at our first meeting he had pinpointed the Crit Champs as one of his major goals for the season. Victory was well within his compass and if achieved, it would bring him the opportunity to wear the red, white and blue jersey of a British national champion. Also in career terms, success here would be a major boost and could have a positive bearing on his attempts to gain a contract with a division one or two team.

Tom's prospects in the race had been improved by the fact that many of the other potential favourites for the event, including the previous year's winner Russell Downing, were missing due to a clash of dates with the Irish Milk Ras and the World Track Championships in Australia. Tom was one of only three continent-based riders that had come back to contest the race and so in many ways he would be a marked man in a distinctly domestic and local field. In contrast, a good number of the riders were regular competitors at Hillingdon and so knew the circuit much better than he did. However, their local knowledge was to an extent offset by the fact that the race was being run in the opposite direction to the normal Tuesday evening events held there. On another positive note, Tom, by dint of his commitments abroad, had been regularly racing at a higher standard than he could expect to find in this event. In short, the title was very much up for grabs.

Now a novice road racer in my own right, I had decided to compete in a short event for inexperienced riders on the same morning as the Crit Champs and so had journeyed down on Saturday (after riding a fifty mile road race in the morning), spending the evening with my brother again in Camden. A major part of my motivation in taking up road racing was to be able to fully understand and comprehend the racing experiences that Graham and Tom generously shared with me. Only by trying to get away in a lone escape, or by chasing down a break, would I understand the strengths and skills that it took to be a competitive bike rider. Of course, my exploits were at a much lower level than those of my two subjects, but they quickly gave me a much better awareness of the nuances and strategies involved in riding a bike at high speed as part of a bunch. A particularly telling lesson that I learnt early on is that the strongest rider does not always win. This is in stark contrast to time-trailing (a discipline in which riders go off at one minute intervals and ride alone) in which on 99.9% of occasions the strongest will win. Road racing, however, has a large number of variables that can influence the outcome, such as the willingness of riders to co-operate with each other, or conversely their willingness to sacrifice their own chances in the name of stopping someone else from winning.

My race began at 10am and so I arrived with Julia and my brother at around nine. Our journey west took us out through some of the landmark sites of London such as Regents Park, but the scene of the Hillingdon circuit was in marked contract to the glamorous locations that we had driven past. The entrance to the circuit was down a quiet road leading to an industrial estate and could easily be missed by the unsuspecting visitor. Once inside, the conditions for the riders were spartan. Toilets, changing and registration took place in two heavily fortified portacabins and there were no showers on site. My initial thought was that this was an unusual and somewhat unambitious choice of venue for a race of national importance.

The circuit in contrast was in good condition. At just under one mile in length it consisted of two long straights and a number of sweeping bends. As I learned when warming up for my race, it was possible to ride a whole lap without touching the brakes. This though was not the kind of circuit that Tom wanted. Instead he would have favoured an urban street-based course, similar in nature to the ones in Belgium on which he regularly raced Kermesses. The layout at Hillingdon meant that it would be difficult to disappear up the road and out of the sight of the field. If the race had been in a town centre, the sharp corners and buildings would act as an aid to a lone attacker, but here the group would always know how far away they were from the front of the field.

Despite the relatively gentle nature of the circuit, I was to experience the inherent dangers of cycle racing at first hand that morning. A touch of wheels during a prime (pronounced 'preem' –

a sprint held for small amounts of money at the end of designated laps) led to a major crash that resulted in a number of casualties and three riders eventually departing for hospital in ambulances. In fact, the blood was being washed off the track at the same time as the casualties were being tended to and although I hadn't been involved in the crash, this was enough to persuade me (and more importantly Julia) that my race for the day was at an end. A small number of committed and success-hungry riders hung around for forty minutes at which point it was decided to conclude the race over a reduced six laps distance, but I was making my way back to the changing rooms when the flag went down once again. In fact I had just reached the portacabins as the Barras family mobile home came into view, struggling to get through the narrow entrance to the circuit.

I made my way over to Tom, who was helping his Dad manoeuvre the vehicle through the narrow gates. It was immediately obvious that he was nervous and I figured that this stemmed from the awareness that his chances were good and of the potential benefits that a win could bring about. After getting changed and enquiring about the injured from my own race, and with the motor home now safely parked by the circuit, I went back to Tom and we resumed our conversation. Over the past couple of weeks I found, he had begun to tailor his training specifically for this race. This had included high-speed sessions conducted behind a motorcycle. These were designed to mimic the effects of riding a Crit and to get some necessary speed into his legs. Despite his nerves, the preparations had gone well and he arrived at the start line in good form.

The race itself was characterised by a number of groups attempting to break away over the early laps. However, each move was successfully chased down and Tom was often prominent in these counter-attacks. To the onlooking crowd, he undoubtedly looked to be one of the strongest riders in a field of widely varying levels of ability, and there were many riders that were happy just to sit in the group and to get round. Tom later noted this unevenness to be in contrast to the racing on the continent, when the gap between the best and worst in a race was generally much smaller.

Without the support of his team, he had to ride hard to keep himself in contention and this was energy sapping work. Many of the other riders had noted Tom's presence and were more than happy to sit on his wheel, knowing that he was a key player and that he could not afford to let a group get away if he was to have a chance of victory. In the end, these efforts took their toll and Tom was unable to go with the decisive break. Faced with the prospect of chasing the lead group of relatively unheralded riders once more, only to see his hard work potentially exploited by other chasers, Tom was left to concede defeat. He finished the race in the second group and was eventually given 13th place. A major chance for a headline-grabbing victory had gone begging and the new champion was 40-year-old Colin Roshier, one of the local riders in the race. On reflection, Tom had in part been a victim of his own high expectations and of being a big fish in a fairly small pond. Again, one of the key factors of road racing had reared its head. A rider often needs more than just strength and determination in order to win.

Following the podium presentation to Roshier, Greg Sandy and Rob Enslin who were second and third respectively, we packed up our belongings and made our way once more to the mobile home. Tom was sitting in the front of the vehicle and his disappointment was there for all to see. One could sense that he didn't really want to talk and again I was in two minds about whether to push things. In the end I tapped on the window and Tom wound it down. I commiserated with him and he began to share his feelings and thoughts about the race with me. This was a generous gesture as in his own words he was gutted.

Careers in sport are built on hard work and talent, but the element of good fortune should not be overlooked. Tom had been strong enough on the day to achieve success, but the race had just not gone for him. This was not to take anything away from the first three who deserved the plaudits that they received. However, it occurred to me that it is particularly difficult to win a bike race when you are one of the favourites, but don't have the support of a team to work for you. It is unlikely, for example, that the field would have let a break go off down the road on that day, had Tom been in it, and the presence of one or two team-mates would have reduced the amount of chasing that he had to do. A positive postscript to the day, however, was that Tom was now going home to Yorkshire with the family that night and was not heading back to Belgium for a couple of days. A heavy workload awaited him on his return to the continent, including a training camp in the Ardennes and a mountainous stage race in Spain. However, before this he would be able to sample some home comforts and to see Liv once again.

Following the presentation to the winner, the small crowd began to clear and Julia and I returned to the car. After our long day in the bright sunlight Julia and I were both tired and a long Sunday evening drive lay ahead of us. As we made our way towards the M25 we couldn't help thinking that Tom was not really receiving the rewards that his talent merited. I had seen him ride three times now, and on each occasion he had impressed me with his strength and tenacity on the bike. However, in some ways, a full season of solid rides were of less use than one single victory or podium placing and this, as we had seen in turn, owes much to chance and how the events unfolded in a race. Who works, the wheel that you follow and simply being in the right place at the right time all play their part in deciding a rider's success or failure. I just hoped that at some point in the season he would experience his day in the sun.

Some hours later we reached home, but my day was still not at an end. A few weeks earlier I been put in touch with Phil Ingham, the Press Officer of the British Cycling Federation, and after talking I had offered to write a report of the race for the BCF website. Again this was a new departure for me, but it meant that I would be burning the midnight oil on my return to Ramsbottom. I made a coffee, switched on the computer and began to rifle through the copious notes I had made during the race. I then began to tell the story of Colin Roshier's victory, finally topping it off with the somewhat corny headline of 'It's Critical for Colin'. I mailed the report to Phil and stumbled off to bed. I can't remember the time, but I do recall thinking that life was suddenly full to almost bursting point. Well I thought, curling up in bed, you asked for it.

CHAPTER 7

The Ras

FOLLOWING HIS EARLY season win in Paris–Evreaux, expectations of Graham were high. His team managers at UC Beauvais Oise were aware that they had a talented rider on their hands and unsurprisingly wanted to get the most from him that they could. However, in the weeks following his first success on foreign soil, Graham's form began to dip and he was unable to sustain the momentum he had generated in his first weeks in France. So whereas March had started with an almighty bang, it faded out with something of a whimper.

Over the horizon in early April, however, was a four-day UCI sanctioned stage race in Belgium, where he would be riding as part of the Great Britain under-23 team. The race, the Tryptique Des Monts was part of the Espoirs World Cup series, an age restricted competition in which national teams from around the world and development squads from some of the big professional teams take part. Graham flew back to the UK from France at the start of the month to meet up with the squad before, ironically, heading back over the Channel to Belgium for the race. For Graham, riding for Great Britain was, although an honour, not the straightforwardly positive event that one might expect it to be. The reason was that it brought back memories of 2003 and his non-selection for the Under-23 Academy – a development that was in a large part responsible for him having to move abroad to forge his career in France. The decision was in some ways hard to swallow for Graham, as it was not based on fears about his ability, but on the grounds of his age and to a lesser extent on his lack of experience as a track rider: both things that he could do nothing about.

The decision to create an Under-23 Academy was motivated by a desire to offer a structured development programme to some of the leading young riders in the country, and competition to join it was fierce. The Academy was to be based in Manchester and all the selected riders were expected to move there, where they would be offered a mixture of training and racing (road and on the track), feedback and analysis, as well as educational elements such as French lessons and courses in bike maintenance and mechanics. The men behind the Academy, such as the under-23 team manager Simon Lillistone and the coach Rod Ellingworth, had decided early on that it would be structured into two 2-year blocks. The first block of the programme was aimed at riders between the ages of 18 and 20 and Graham, who was already 20 at this point, was judged to be just too old to qualify. By all accounts he was devastated at the news. However, after a period of reflection he swallowed his disappointment and decided to move on by applying for (and receiving the support of) the Fund and then in turn by linking up with his present club in France. It was good to know that despite not making the Academy, Graham remained in the thoughts of the managers of the national team, and his selection for events like the Tryptique Des Monts allowed them to continue to monitor his progress and in return it offered Graham a chance to represent his country and to maintain a relationship with the other members of the squad.

Graham returned home to Doncaster for a few days after the race and it was there that I caught him for a quick telephone conversation. He told me about the race itself and from his reactions it had clearly been a mixed experience for him. In the first stage, which was over 160 kilometres in length, his great sprinting ability earned him a highly creditable 9th place. This made him the leading British rider in the race at that point. The second stage was a time-trial on the following day and as he was the reigning British Espoirs circuit time-trial champion, this should have given him a further opportunity to shine. However, his chances of doing well were dealt a significant blow when it was realised that the team had not brought a small version of the low profile, aerodynamic time-trial bikes that they were to use on the stage. This left Graham with the choice of either using a bike that was quick but too big for him, or of riding the time-trial on his normal road bike. In the end he plumped for the road bike, but he was at a great disadvantage to the other competitors and it was no surprise that he finished well down the field. The third stage brought even more bad luck as he crashed and in the end he suffered the disappointment of not being able to complete the race. In a period of just over a month, Graham had experienced the highs and lows, the pleasures and the pains that characterise competitive bike racing. The overall winner of the race was Thomas Dekker from Holland, who was riding for the Rabobank (division 1 professional team) development squad. Dekker was already being spoken of as a special rider and it was noted in the press at that time that he was fresh from duelling with and in fact beating Lance Armstrong in another early season race.

Back home in South Yorkshire, Graham was able to spend some time with his family and with Sam. However, it was a fairly manic period and he felt the pressure here too, having to catch up with a large number of people in a short space of time. All this was on top of being tired and bruised from his crash in the third stage of the race. After a few days at home, he caught another flight and was on his way back to the team house in Beauvais. Now though, there were four in the house as Graham, Caspar and Dimitri had been joined by another young Moldovan rider, Vladimir, who had just joined the team.

During the remainder of April, Graham's form returned in fits and starts and on a couple of good days he was able to place second and fifth in two domestics races in France. Conversely, he also failed to finish on a number of occasions during this time. However, potentially as damaging as a loss of form was the fact that relations in the team house were beginning to deteriorate. Some of the other members of the team, including Caspar and Dimitri, saw what they thought were elements of selfishness in Graham's riding and they were concerned that he did not do enough work for his team-mates, such as riding on the front of the group to bring back a breakaway. Graham acknowledged that he could see how they had come to this conclusion, but denied that there was any truth to their negative image of him. He was clear that he was not just out for himself and wanted to explain this to them. The language barriers did not help here, but he tried to make his case that such lapses were due in part to his relative inexperience on the bike (he had only been riding seriously since the age of 17). The others had been competing for much longer than Graham and had a deeper and more instinctive knowledge of how to read a race, as well as a well-developed appreciation of the etiquette of the peloton. Rather than knowingly ignoring the needs of his team-mates, Graham was sometimes guilty of not judging a particular situation in the way that a fully-schooled rider would. This though, was part of the reason that he was in France: to learn how to race and make the right decisions in a pressure cooker environment.

In addition, everyone agreed that Graham's greatest strength as a rider was in the final sprint and this meant that it would be foolish for him to blunt his high-end speed working hard to drag the bunch around. He reasoned, and with some justification, that there would be no point in wearing himself out before the business end of the race and he knew that the ability to sprint is a highly valuable commodity in professional cycling and can be the difference between a solid and a glittering career. Very often even a long race will be won by the man with the best final furlong gallop and it is pointless for riders such as this to expend too much energy by fulfilling the role of the worker ant.

Results are ultimately what counts in professional sport, and Graham's value to this and future teams would be higher than that of others simply by virtue of his powerful sprint finish. It wasn't fair, and it would not be welcome news to such riders, but who ever said that professional sport is fair? In football not everyone can be the centre-forward; in the same way not all cyclists can be the sprint king. Also, in a fully-fledged professional team the roles and responsibilities of the different team members are usually more clearly defined. However, in a club team such as UC Beauvais Oise, things would not be as formalised and any hierarchies that developed would be more likely to be enforced by the riders themselves.

Despite Graham's ongoing protestations, things became so bad that at one point some of the team members stopped talking to each other (in any of their respective languages) and as a result the cohesion of the team was for a time threatened. However, everyone knew deep down that this was not a sustainable situation and that they would all ultimately lose out if things continued in the same way. Consequently a rapprochement was eventually reached and the housemates began to work together again both on and off the bike. For example, Graham helped Dimitri with his English and in turn Dimitri helped Graham with his French. In fact, from having no French on the day he landed at Charles de Gaulle airport, Graham was now in a position to hold conversations in the language and unlike his colleagues from the Under-23 Academy, Graham's French had not been learned in the classroom, but in France with all the contextual advantages that this would bring.

April moved into May and although the weather began to become warmer Graham was struck down by illness. This prevented him from competing in the Tour de Loiret and was not good preparation for his forthcoming next appearance in the red, white and blue colours of the Great Britain under-23s in the FDB Milk Ras in Ireland. The Ras as it is commonly known, is the National Tour of Ireland and has been in existence since 1953. It takes place over 8 days that see the route pass through some of the most scenic countryside in Ireland, before ending with a short stage in Phoenix Park in Dublin. The Ras has a special place in cycling mythology, due in no small part to the range of teams that are able to take part. For example, the 2004 event saw professional teams from Slovenia, Germany and the USA involved, but at the other extreme it also witnessed a team from the Liverpool Century amateur club in England in the field. Such diversity is added to by the inclusion in the race of a number of Irish teams representing a range of different counties and as a result there are many different races within the Ras. Also, many of the competitors although talented riders are not full-time cyclists and have to take time off from their jobs to compete, so for some the main goal is simply to finish the race.

Having corresponded by email with Sam, it was agreed that we would go over to Dublin for the final weekend of the Ras and that we would meet Graham at the team hotel on the morning of the final stage for a chat before heading off to watch the Crit in Phoenix Park. Sam told us that she would be travelling to Dublin with Graham's parents and this was an added bonus for me, as I had long looked forward to the opportunity of meeting them and seeing how they viewed Graham's burgeoning career as a cyclist.

As soon as it was confirmed that Graham would be taking part in the race, I made one of my regular trips to the websites of the no-frills airlines. After a little digging I found a reasonably priced flight and this time Julia and I would be flying to Dublin from Blackpool on Saturday lunchtime and would return on the following Monday, which was a Bank Holiday in England. Having made the booking I realised that we would be following our visit to London to see Tom in the British Crit Champs with another long journey over the following weekend. However, for my part I was nothing but excited at the prospect. This after all was part of living the life that I craved when I had been ill.

The week of the Ras came and I was able to keep up to date with each day's developments via the excellent official website that had been set up for the week of the event. Each day I would quietly log on to the site at around 4.30pm whilst at work, to read the stage results and to look for Graham's name. Things began well and I was pleased to see G. Briggs near the top of the list on a number of the early days. His form, it seemed, had returned and he was more than holding his own against the more vaunted riders in the race. The Ras was turning into a solid performance, but just when he could begin to see the end, things went badly wrong. The penultimate stage was from Carrick-on-Suir to Tullow – a hilly 149 kilometres – and he suffered badly in the hills, losing nearly an hour on the field. Such bad days are every stage racer's nightmare, when a week or more of good results can be wiped out on one energy-sapping stage. Despite the pain Graham hung on, however, and although he was well down the field he completed the stage in the knowledge that the race was almost done and dusted. Sunday's Crit was only a flat 40 kilometres and although the pace would be high he was nearly home. What's more, he was likely to be stronger for having completed the Ras and this could bring rewards in his subsequent races.

After a short flight from Blackpool we arrived in Dublin and spent an enjoyable Saturday seeing the sights and dodging the myriad hen-parties that were having a wild weekend in and around the Temple Bar area. Sunday, however, was the main event for me and I was nervous and excited at the same time as we set off in a taxi to the West County Hotel in the Chapelizod area of the city where Graham and the rest of the team were staying. Indeed this was the Race HQ for the stage and as we pulled into the car park of the hotel it was clear that it had been overtaken by the travelling circus that is a stage race.

Entering the foyer, we saw Sam almost immediately and although it was raining and overcast outside, her smile of recognition and that given in return by Julia seemed to light up the room. Graham was having his pre-race meal with the rest of the team and so we began the process of catching up in his absence. After a while he joined us, looking tanned and healthy, but he displayed a degree of edginess that was easily attributable to nerves. I smiled at this, because although having nothing like Graham's talent I could match if not beat him for pre-race irritability. This was in contrast to some of the more experienced professionals in the race who were siting on a nearby sofa. Their demeanour signaled the fact that they had seen all this many times before. Indeed one or two well-known members of the field were happily discussing the merits of the bar in which they had spent the previous evening, thereby destroying some more of my remaining naïve views of the hermit-like lifestyle of the dedicated cyclist.

Despite his distracted state, Graham was able to tell me that he was due to fly back to Beauvais almost immediately after the race. In fact, so small was the window between the end of the race and his departure time from Dublin airport that a top three placing in the stage and the resulting podium presentation and drugs control would put his ability to catch his flight in jeopardy. What a position, I thought. Having to balance ambition against simply getting home. Graham was soon off again, this time to change into his kit before going out on the road to warm up with the rest of the team. Whilst he was away, Graham's erstwhile mentor, Kevin Dawson came past our table after signing on for the stage and joined us, or more precisely, Sam for a chat. Kevin, or just Kev as he is known throughout the sport, is another native of Doncaster and a fine road racer in his own right. As well as this, he is a multiple winner of the prestigious Best British Allrounder award for time-trialling performance over a number of distances. Kev had been a team-mate of Graham's with Life Repair in 2003, but their friendship pre-dates this and he had played an instrumental part in him getting a ride on the team. As this suggests, their relationship is a close one. They were regular winter training partners as well as friends and although they were riding for different teams in the Ras it was clear that Kev was still keen to help Graham whenever he could, even looking out for him during the race itself. What was also clear was Kev's friendship with and affection for Sam and it was another indication of the close ties that exist within the sport. In fact, looking around the lounge of the hotel I was impressed by the number of family members that were happily chatting away to the fully kitted-up bike riders that would soon be tearing around the park.

Graham's family had headed straight to the park from their hotel and we were due to meet them there. So Sam, Julia and I shared a final 'good luck' with the now wet Graham and went off to order a taxi to get us to the park before the race arrived. The journey to Phoenix Park was only short, but the taxi driver and more precisely his strident views on drugs in the sport meant that it was a lively ride. Unsurprisingly, he was a total cynic, believing that all current and past top cyclists used some or other perform-ance enhancing substance. This was a slightly depressing counterpoint to the race, but was another reminder of the way in which the sport is regarded by sections of the public. At the same time, however, I had to remember that taxi drivers the world over seem to have a negative yet encyclopedic knowledge of almost any subject and can complain and bemoan ad nauseum. Maybe, I thought as we closed the doors of the taxi behind us, and as I remembered the trip in from the airport on the previous day, when we had been treated to a diatribe on illegal immigration in Ireland by another driver, they aren't that typical after all.

Once free of the attentions of the taxi driver, we began to wander up one of the park's wide avenues towards the finishing line and it was here that we met Graham's Mum and Dad, Denise and Rob, together with an Aunt and Uncle that had also made the trip over for the end of the Ras. Graham's Dad was intrigued by our presence and was keen to know what had moved me to spend a year following his son around Europe in the name of writing a book. This was an invitation for me to recount the whole Cheeky Phil story once more. Re-telling the various episodes that had been the genesis of the book once more, served as a reminder of how far along the project we now were and how much fun and fulfillment I had gained from it. Conscious of talking too much, I cut short the story to ask him what he thought of his son's adventure in cycling. Rob was obviously proud, but at the same time was understated in his appreciation of his son. However, the more he talked, the more it became clear that it was Graham's overall welfare that moved his parents the most and that I thought was the way it should be. Too many people try to live out their own dreams through their children and it was reassuring to know that this wasn't the case with Graham's parents. Rob wasn't just proud in a fatherly way, but he was also impressed at an objective level by the commitment Graham had shown to chasing his dream. Sam, too was commended for her dedication and support and once again the team of Briggs and MacInnes was seen in a very positive light.

At this point the riders appeared at the end of the avenue. They were not yet at racing speed as the race was still neutralised. A sizeable crowd was now in place and the rain had abated, and as they came across the finishing line for the first of two controlled laps we looked out for Graham in the bunch. It was good to see him racing and it struck me that this was the first time I had actually seen him on a bike.

The following hour was taken up with multiple laps of the park, interspersed with a number of primes. Towards the end the speed began to increase noticeably and it was clear that the GB Under-23s were making a concerted attempt to take control of the stage.

By the time the field entered the finishing straight for the penulti-mate time the first five positions were occupied by the team and it was Graham that was at the head of the race driving it along as the bell was sounded for the start of the final lap. The sight of the GB train at the head of the field, with Graham head down punching away on the front, became one of my abiding memories of the year. The fact that Julia, who was on camera duty that day, managed to capture the image in all its drama and spectacle, only added to its significance for me. Here also was a welcome retort to those who thought Graham was not a team player. He, alongside three other members of the team, had been tasked with keeping the pace high for Mark Cavendish, the rider nominated to go for the final sprint that day. His work done and with fatigue setting in, Graham dropped off the pace as the field went down the back straight for the final time and he coasted across the line a few seconds after Mark and the other leaders and after a nasty-looking crash had taken care of a number of riders.

The Ras was now at an end, but in what was by now a recurring theme, Graham did not have long to spend with Sam and his family before he (and his bike) had to be transported to the airport. There was just enough time for a quick goodbye and then they were heading back to the cars before setting off for home. We said our goodbyes and began to walk through Phoenix Park towards a bus stop and our ride back to the centre of Dublin. At this point the clouds cleared and the sun came out and it was suddenly a warm summer's day.

During our stroll we reflected on another great day, but also on how Graham's resolve was now being put under some strain. Perhaps, I thought, his early success had proved to be a mixed blessing. At the same time as making an instant impression, Paris–Evreaux had turned him into something of a marked man, even within his own team. In addition, the management now (somewhat unrealistically) expected him to turn in that kind of performance every week. Things had now become tougher and he would be sure to feel the lack of a network of support more keenly. However, it would be times like this, when the novelty of being in a new environment had begun to wear off and when results were harder to come by, when Graham would really learn what it is to be a professional cyclist. Faced with this realisation, our admiration for him simply grew stronger. The temptation to come home must have been strong, especially after competing in the Ras, where he had been surrounded for a week by familiar faces such as Kev Dawson and where he had been reunited with Sam and his parents. If it had been me, I'm pretty sure that I wouldn't have had the courage and strength to go to the airport in order to take the flight back to Beauvais. If it had been me, I would have told the driver of the team car to keep going to the ferry terminal where a boat to England was waiting. But then, this is the sort of thing that separates the committed athlete from the dilettante, the winner from the also-ran: that sheer bloody-mindedness that allows one to endure, to keep going when a part of yourself wants very much to give in. It is easy to relate to the scenario during a race, but here was a young man of twenty experiencing it in life and I was proud to think that despite the hardships – or maybe because of them – Graham was displaying an inner strength in spades.

Monday was another fine day, but we didn't have time to enjoy Dublin. Instead we headed for the airport and our return flight. Again we were surrounded by hen parties galore, but their weekend frolics had obviously tired them out and they were hardly noticeable, apart from their large green leprechaun hats of course. Julia and I sat on the aircraft and as we flew past Blackpool Tower on our final descent into the tiny airport, we mused once more on just how exciting the year was becoming. However, although it seemed petty to complain, the situation was not without some complication. How, for example would I explain our latest set of exploits when someone at work half-heartedly asked me what I had got up to at the weekend. Working with Graham and Tom was taking me out of my 'old' life and into uncharted waters and it was true that some people found the change a little too much to handle. I had in consequence to admit that in some conversations I was beginning to play the whole thing down. I was worried that some people wouldn't believe me and that the ones that did would think that I was having too much fun. However, at the same time I also knew deep down that there is no such concept as too much fun.

CHAPTER 8

A Mission Accomplished

WITH THE SEASON in full swing it was sometimes difficult to maintain contact with Graham and Tom. Both had busy itineraries and were often away from their summer bases. However, the end of June brought both back to the UK once again, this time to compete in the National Road Race Championships at the Celtic Manor resort in South Wales. The Nationals are the pinnacle of the sport in this country and by 2004 were also something of a meeting point for the top British riders, with so many of them now based on the continent.

The event also had a personal resonance for me as it was two years ago at this very event, (when held at Rivington), that I had first seen Cheeky Phil, resplendent in the colours of UC Briquebec. The anniversary was also significant for what it said about my own journey. I was now mostly healthy and in my own small way a racing cyclist, which was enough, even without the ongoing adventure of viewing the season through the prism of Graham and Tom.

I was therefore very happy to be travelling down the M5 in heavy rain on the day before the race. Whilst not exactly complacent, I had now stopped pinching myself at the prospect of going to major bike races, so, it was nice to have a different companion in the car for the weekend. Toni Mion is a long-standing cycling buddy of mine, whose parents came over from

Italy many years ago and who grew up, and indeed stills lives, in the grounds of one of Cheshire's stately homes (where his Mum and Dad were part of the staff of the landowning gentry that live at the Hall). Toni displays some quintessentially Italian qualities, such as a love of bikes, cycling and women and at the same time possesses a chronic indecisiveness seemingly designed exclusively to test the patience of the likes of me. However, he is also an English touring cyclist to his core, with a love of quiet lanes and Ordnance Survey maps that would not be out of place in the poetry of Betjeman.

We were in good spirits as we set off from Stockport, but our journey took place in gloomy conditions and with a significant cloud hanging over the event. Almost inevitably it concerned doping. David Millar, the main reason for my visit to Rivington two years ago and incidentally the first rider to receive the support of the Dave Rayner Fund, had been embroiled all year in a drugs scandal that had hit his French Cofidis team. Always protesting his innocence and appearing to be something of a sporting enigma with a prodigious talent and an equally large love of life, Millar struck many people as almost the last member of the peloton that would stoop to take performance-enhancing drugs. However, in the week of the Nationals a story broke in the press that he had confessed to taking EPO.

On the Tuesday before our trip to Wales, Millar had been visited by French detectives whilst out having dinner with friends in his adopted home town of Biarritz. The police, who were investigating allegations made by another member of the Cofidis team, had searched his apartment and had allegedly found empty containers of Eprex (one of the commercial brands of EPO) hidden inside a book. Millar had been whisked away for questioning and again at this stage only allegedly, had confessed to taking the banned substance in 2001 and then twice more in 2003, including once in Manchester as he prepared for the World Championship time-trial that he went on to win.

This was a man that Roger Hammond and Jeremy Hunt simply knew as Dave. I remembered back to eating pizza with them and Tom, Matt Brindle and Hilton Clarke at Easter and wondering, Who is this 'Dave' guy that they're talking about? –

before putting two and two together and quickly removing the look of surprise from my face. David Millar was their friend and pretty soon he was due to be a team-mate of Roger and Jez in the British Olympic team in Athens. Luckily, for all concerned he had already decided before the story broke not to ride the Nationals and was due instead to be elsewhere honing his preparations for the Tour de France. Now, though, his participation in that event was in doubt, as was his very future as a professional.

In the past, the events of the week would have brought about a sense of moral indignation on my part, but now I just felt sad. I was sad that the Dave Rayner Fund would lose its major success story, sad that Roger and Jez would lose a talented team-mate, sad that the sport had yet more bad publicity and ultimately sad for David Millar himself. I had never met him and almost all my knowledge of him came from TV broadcasts and newspaper articles. However, to me he brought a certain élan and panache to all he did in the sport, although it has to be said that this was not always in a constructive way. However, for me anyone that can ride up one of the most intimidating mountains in the Tour of Spain (the Angliru) and then simply climb off the bike yards before the end of the stage, in protest at the conditions and organisation of the race, has something of the romantic about them.

I remembered the clamor that surrounded Millar's bravura act at the Vuelta. Old professionals were quick to criticise, accusing him of a lack of professionalism, but I saw it differently. Here was someone who rode his bike because he loved it, not just because it was a job. Someone who had a passion for what they did. Not the kind of person that embodied the cynic's views of sporting professionalism as the home of the calculating cheat. So what made him do it? Why did he dope himself? That for me is the key question. Not what did he take and how did he take it, but why? What drove him, what pressures bore down on him to force him to in his own words, live a lie?

Toni and I were booked into college Halls of Residence in the village of Caerleon for the weekend. I expected that the site would be full of cyclists and their supporters, eager to exploit the cheap and convenient accommodation. It was somewhat surprising, therefore, when we arrived to find that there were only around three other people on site. One of these, however, was Tom's team-mate from Cyclingnews.com, Hamish Haynes.

Earlier in the week I had been in contact with both Graham and Tom to find out how and when they were getting to Newport and what their expectations were. Not wanting to interfere with their pre-race preparation I arranged to meet both of them after the race itself by the big screen that was to be erected to broadcast the event. Graham was travelling back to Doncaster in the middle of the week, where he was due to spend some time at home before heading south on Saturday with Sam. They were booked into a hotel in Cheltenham on the night before the race and were due to drive across on the Sunday morning. Graham's goal was simply to finish the race. The biggest challenge that he would face in the UK in the year would be the Under-23 Championships. This was not until July and I suspected that part of his reason for entering the Nationals was to have the opportunity to escape for a while from the demands of France and to re-assess his training and goals for the rest of the season.

Tom on the other hand was travelling by car with Roger straight to Newport. Both Roger and Jez were booked into the Celtic Manor hotel, in recognition of the first and third places they had respectively achieved in the previous year's race. For Tom, however, the night before the race would be spent at a nearby beauty spot in the more humble surroundings of the Barras family motorhome. Tom saw his role in the race partly as that of unofficial domestique (or worker) for Roger and Jez, despite the fact that he rode for a different team to them. It was not necessarily what his bosses in Belgium would have wanted, but it was a practical way of repaying the favours that the other two had done him over the season, in terms of accommodation and transport to races. This tells us much about the mutual support that goes on in the peloton and how it can transcend pure team loyalties.

On our own arrival on Saturday afternoon, Toni and I had

decided to go for a ride on our bikes. We first rode up to the Celtic Manor Resort and then simply followed the large arrowed signs to embark on a lap of the course. I recall thinking at the time that this is one of the great things about cycling. Unlike Wembley or Wimbledon where the turf is hallowed and off-limits to the public, anyone can take a spin on the roads used by the best bike riders in the world. We followed the signs for some distance and encountered exhilarating descents and challenging climbs, before heading back to the resort, where to my surprise I found Tom in the foyer of the hotel. He and Roger had just arrived and Roger was checking into the hotel. We had a quick conversation and it was an interesting reversal in roles for me to be in full cycling kit and for Tom to be asking me how I'd been going. I was now, after all, in possession of a full 4 BFC points and was on the verge of reaching the heady heights of being a third category road racer. I mentioned to Tom that Hamish was staying at the same place as us and he told us that Hamish had only decided to make the trip to the race at the last possible moment and had made his own way across from Belgium.

After saying goodbye, I went outside to find Toni having of all things, a miniature TV camera strapped to his bike. An independent production company, it appeared, were making a series of short films on cycling, to be shown over the three weeks of the Tour de France. One of these was on the brilliantly talented Welsh cyclist Nicole Cooke and she had competed in and won that day's Women's Road Race. Shaun, the young and enthusiastic director, was keen to have some shots taken from a racing bike that he could cut into the film and so Toni, who was standing around waiting for me whilst I spoke to Tom, had volunteered to be the guinea pig. The next thirty minutes were taken up with the camera being positioned on various parts of the bike before Toni would ride off at high speed through the golf course and back again. It seemed that my world of bizarre coincidence was spreading to affect other people and the remainder of the weekend was only to reinforce this impression.

Having finished his filming duties for the day, Toni and I headed off back to the Halls and it was here that we first encountered Hamish, sitting in the kitchen, heating up a cauliflower cheese and going slowly mad with boredom. There was no television or radio or even any books in the building and it seemed that for him the night before the race was going to be a long one. We introduced ourselves and I mentioned the fact that I was working with Tom to document his season. As we began to talk, Hamish confirmed what Tom had told us. An early season disrupted by sickness had left him short of form, but he decided to take a gamble and return for the race. In fact, the decision was so late in the day that he had to travel back alone and via a highly circuitous route. A drive to Amsterdam (courtesy of a team-mate) was followed by a flight to Bristol. He then took the train to Newport before unpacking his race bike and riding the last miles to the Halls. Luckily, I was able to furnish him with that week's copy of Cycling Weekly to while away the time whilst his cauliflower cheese cooked.

Despite the improvised travelling arrangements, Hamish was certainly up for the race, going so far as to say what he'd do if he won. This was in contrast to both Tom and Graham who for their own different reasons did not really expect to challenge for honours. However, if he was to figure, Hamish needed someone to look after his feeds during the race and to pass him his bottles as it went on. Toni and I almost instantly volunteered for the job, without really understanding what we had to do. We were now going to be actually involved in the race as impromptu soigneurs and not just as mere spectators. We arranged to meet him back in the kitchen at 9am on Sunday morning and left him to tuck into his microwave meal and magazine. Feeling somewhat guilty we headed out for dinner and a few drinks and more importantly to discuss our roles and responsibilities for the following day.

Sunday dawned free from the torrential rain of the previous day and I made my way to the kitchen to find Toni and Hamish in conversation. We ate breakfast and Hamish began to prepare himself for the race. We were to take his belongings and food by car to the Celtic Manor whilst he rode across. By 10am we were parked up on the golf course complex and began to look out for Tom and Graham. Finding Tom is never difficult when he travels with his Mum and Dad (due to the size of their motorhome) and I was quickly able to introduce him to Toni as he prepared his bike for the race.

We then made our way over to the start to wait for Hamish to arrive and to watch the riders sign on. Standing in the morning sunshine, I was impressed by the sight before me. The plush surroundings of the Celtic Manor, the helicopter buzzing overhead, the big screen, as well as the large number of Europe-based riders mulling around outside the hotel, made for a glamorous spectacle. Rivington had not been like this and things certainly seemed to have moved on in the last two years. As well as the sporting context, one of the things that struck me was the relaxed and sociable atmosphere of the pre-race build up. For many riders, especially those living abroad, this would be one of the few times in the year when they would be reunited with their friends and in some instance ex-team-mates and it was nice to see so many people just catching up with each other. This made me think that despite the seemingly singular nature of their sport, it would be way off the mark to think that there was no camaraderie between bike riders. At one point, Tom's friend Matt passed us on the way to sign on for the race and we wished him luck and again it was nice to think that there was another person in the race that we could shout for.

As the start time approached I was aware that I hadn't yet seen Graham. The thought crossed my mind that for some reason he had decided not to take part, but then at almost the last minute I caught sight of him on the other side of the barriers. He looked nervous and in some ways like he would rather be anywhere else but here, but his face brightened when he saw us and again I wished him the obligatory good luck.

The field rolled out on the first of the three 25-mile long large laps of the circuit and after a short while Toni and I made our way across to the other side of the golf course to the feed zone. It was here where we would soon take up our duties for the day on behalf of Hamish. The race wouldn't come through for up to an hour, but we were determined not to be late. At first we were the only ones there, but as the time grew nearer, more and more people began to congregate in the designated area. It was obvious that many of them were family and friends of the different riders and looking across back to the hotel it seemed that a procession of milkmen was coming our way, with many carrying plastic handled containers designed to take six or eight drinks bottles.

A number of people were complaining about the length of the feed zone (it was apparently too short) and the fact that it was on a slight downhill stretch. I nodded in agreement, without really understanding the implications of their grievance. By this time, Toni and I had split up and were standing at opposite ends of the area in order to give Hamish two chances to grab a musette (the canvas bag containing his drinks bottles). From time to time we looked back towards each other and our determined and nervous expressions were in contrast to the relaxed demeanour of most of the other people there. They had probably done this many times before, but we must have looked like obvious first timers.

After a while the race lead car came past closely followed by the main peloton. The race was still together at this point and it became clear to us now why the location of the feed zone was such an issue. The field sped past at such high speeds as to make it almost impossible to hand up a bottle and I don't recall anyone receiving a feed on the first time around. This led to much disgruntlement among the helpers, but my main memory was watching Roger in the middle of the field eating as he came past and riding with such ease at to make it look as if he was on a Sunday morning potter with his mates. At this point, news began to spread that the race organisers had decided to extend the feed zone outside the grounds of the Celtic Manor and on to the hill that the led up from Caerleon. With this we all trooped away to watch the race on the big screen at the hotel, before re-convening at a slightly different location roughly forty-five minutes later.

Again the race came around and this time the riders were more spread out. Hamish was near the head of the field and as I saw him, I took a step out into the road to hand him his musette. He came past, and as he did, he took his left hand off the bars and in an instant he had taken the bag and in one movement had cast it over his shoulder. A few seconds later and the bottles had been removed from the musette and the bag itself had been thrown away. We had successfully carried out our duties for the first time and now headed back to the big screen with an added sense of accomplishment. It was here that I saw Sam for the first time, talking to John Tanner, a previous winner of the title and one of Graham's ex-Life Repair team-mates, who had already abandoned. I made a mental note to catch her for a chat at the end of the next lap and we proceeded on our way.

Our roles in support of Hamish had to an extent taken my concentration away from Graham and Tom's progress. However, as the race had come past for a second time I became aware that Graham was struggling towards the back of the field. It was no surprise to find out later that he too had abandoned at the end of that lap. Tom, as ever, was riding strongly in the main pack.

Despite his long journey, Hamish was also riding well and as the decisive breakaway group went away on the next lap, he was very much to the fore. Also in the group were Roger, Jez and a number of the other riders based on the continent and it seemed that not many of the home-based contingent were able to live with the pace that was being set at the front. Tom also began to suffer soon after and his race ended when he was ushered into the broom wagon (the van that follows the race and sweeps up riders that in the opinion of the race commissaries have fallen too far behind). By this time, the race had shifted onto a series of shorter finishing laps and we began to be called into action on Hamish's behalf at more regular intervals. We were also joined at this point by Sam and a freshly-changed Graham and we were able to have a good conversation about how things were going in France. At one level, Graham was able to talk positively about his experiences. Life in the house was going well and his relationship with the other team members was blossoming. However, it seemed that the same could not be said for the team bosses, who did not appear to be the best communicators, irrespective of the language barriers. On one or two occasions, for example, Graham was not told in advance that he was racing on a particular day. The first he knew about it was when the managers came to pick him up. This was obviously not the best preparation in the world. After the race, he was due to travel to Doncaster, where he would spend the week back on home ground and one could not escape the fact that Graham was simply glad to be going home and although he did his best in the race, the Nationals were something of a means to an end in this respect.

As the race unfolded Roger's strength took him away from the group, although he had with him a strong-looking Tom Southam. Tom rides in Italy for the Amore e Vita team (translated for me by Toni as the Love and Life team) and is another graduate of the Dave Rayner Fund. This got me thinking, Why do things sounds so much better in Italian? – a notion which only grew when Toni went on to tell me that the great Italian sprinter Mario Chippilini's team, Aqua e Sapone, is in fact the Soap and Water team.

The two leaders were together as the race went into it final stages, but Roger had just enough in the tank to overcome his opponent on the final climb and to win his second consecutive British title. This was a significant achievement because I knew from talking to Tom in Belgium that Roger had been ill during the previous week. To complete the success, Jez was able to sprint away from the chasing group to take third place.

After the race Roger was taken away for numerous press interviews and we caught up with both Tom and Hamish, who we found riding around the golf course looking for the men (i.e. us) that had his kit bag. Tom was sanguine about his day's efforts and like Graham was clearly looking forward to spending some time at home. In fact, for the riders based in Europe, the Nationals seemed like a book-end to one part of the season, with many seemingly making ready to pay a visit to their families. It occurred to me that the pain of Sunday afternoon must have been softened for some by the knowledge of what was to come afterwards.

Hamish told us that he had paid for his early efforts and eventually faded on the tough hills of South Wales. He was finally eliminated with one lap to go and was given a highly creditable 21st place. He was unhappy to be pulled out, though, as due to a mix-up there was a group behind him on the road that was allowed to go on. Despite the disappointment though, he was content with his performance and thought it would accelerate his recent return to form. Deciding to forego the pleasures of two nights alone in the College Halls of Residence, Hamish also decided to take advantage of our offer of a lift back to Manchester to spend some rare time with his Dad, before he traveled back to Belgium. This meant that we had to fit three people as well as three racing bikes into Julia's car: a Renault Megane that I had borrowed for the weekend as my own car was being repaired after a minor motorway shunt. The task was similar to the sort of thing they give to management trainees on Outward Bound courses and I can only conclude that Hamish must be top brass material as it was he who managed to disassemble the bikes to the extent that we were able to ease down the rear door with everything inside and to set off at around 6pm that night.

Over the course of our journey we talked extensively and we were surprised to learn that Hamish hadn't even taken up competitive cycling until the age of 23. Before that he had been a rock climber, but over time, the racing bug had bitten and he joined Manchester Wheelers and then the Stockport-based Wills Wheels RT (whose members I now raced against regularly in the Crit series at the Preston Arena). He then decided to move things up a notch and moved over to Belgium, which was in his view the place to be.

In 2003, looking to advance to the next level, Hamish moved on to Italy, and he and Toni were able to swap stories of walking and riding in the Dolomite mountains. However, things didn't go too well due to team problems and in mid-season he headed back to Belgium. There he hit a rich seam of form that brought 10 amateur wins and a place alongside Tom on the Cyclingnews.com team for 2004. Unlike Tom, Hamish was living in the team house and was sharing a room with Matt Rice and I remembered my brief conversation with him before the GP de Denain. In seemingly no time we had reached the outskirts of Manchester and I dropped off first Toni and then Hamish. Another typical weekend, I mused, as I made the final part of the journey back to Ramsbottom.

I spoke to both Graham and Tom over the following week

that they spent in England. Graham had taken the opportunity to catch up with Kev Dawson and had settled upon a new training plan in an attempt to regain the edge that he felt he had lost over the previous weeks. As we spoke it seemed to me that he had also re-found his sense of purpose and he told me that he was now gearing all his efforts towards a good performance in the Under-23 Championships in July. This would be key to securing a place in the Great Britain team for the European and World Championships later in the year.

In the aftermath of the Nationals, Tom had been joined in Yorkshire by Jez, and the two were putting in training rides across the Dales. In fact when I rang Tom on his mobile, he and Jez were on the bikes and just passing Bolton Abbey on their way to a stop for coffee and a toasted tea-cake. It was nice to know that even top bike riders still go out on semi-recreational rides and I wondered if Premiership footballers ever went for a kick about in the park. Tom told me that Roger, Jez and he would be staying on for a race in the North-East over the following weekend, the Grainger Grand Prix. The idea was to work as a team in order to accomplish something of a smash and grab raid. This they duly achieved, meaning that they all returned to Belguim with slightly fuller wallets. Tom explained to me over the phone as the group were travelling back that overall, the week had been a case of mission accomplished and I felt that this could be said, albeit in different ways, for both he and Graham.

We had now reached the mid-point of the season and out on a bike ride I took the opportunity to look back at how far we had all come. It had been simply brilliant. However, whilst I was aware that to date the story had been overwhelmingly positive I had a gut feeling that it was only a matter of time before one or both of them experienced some kind of misfortune. Of course I didn't want to see Graham or Tom suffer, but I figured that the precarious nature of their chosen occupation meant that disaster could never be far away. What I didn't know at the time though, was how soon my suspicions would be realised.

CHAPTER 9

Running on Empty

THE WORLD OF elite sport is one in which athletes are frequently forced to deal with extremes, both of a physical and an emotional nature. These peaks and troughs are akin to riding a roller coaster and such is the intensity of the experience that often when sportsmen and women return to our mundane world, they struggle to cope with the relative lack of excitement in their lives. July was to be a month in which Graham's experiences could have acted as a case study in the phenomenon.

Following the Nationals, Graham had spent a relaxed and yet significant week at home before heading back to France. He took back with him a clear set of priorities for the remainder of the year, a renewed sense of resolution and an understanding of what it would take to achieve his ambitions. His primary target, as ever, was the National Under-23 Road Race to be held on the 23rd of the month at Oakley in Buckinghamshire. This was a key race against the other aspiring British riders of his generation (including a number that were also being supported by the Fund) and one in which Graham hoped to stamp his authority over his contemporaries. The race also offered an ideal opportunity to send another reminder of his talents to the Great Britain selectors, as after being given initial indications that he would be representing his country at the European championships at the end of the month, the channels of communication with British Cycling had now gone distinctly quiet. As a result, Graham had multiple motivations to do well in the race.

Once back in France, he began working hard on and off the bike in order to lose some of the unwanted extra kilos that had been put on over the course of the season. Some bike riders, like Tom for instance, struggle to maintain their weight during the racing season, but Graham's constitution is different and like many of us, he has an ongoing battle with his weight. This in turn meant that he had to fight the urge to eat when unhappy or simply just bored. However, in addition there was added pressure in that his weight had a direct bearing on his perceived ability to do his job and in how he was seen by other riders and by his team managers.

At the same time, he attempted to move back to a more regulated training programme, to ensure that he would arrive at the start of the race in Oakley in peak condition. One of the difficulties that he had found during the year was a seeming lack of structure to his week and this meant that it was not always easy for him to train effectively (in contrast to the previous year when he was based at home). Now though, he was determined to try to re-create some of the conditions that had allowed him to be so successful in 2003 and earlier on in 2004.

To the uninitiated, cycling often means only one thing and that is the Tour de France. The race takes place over three weeks in July, before the traditional French holiday season begins, and it alternates between moving around the country in a clockwise direction in one year and then in an anti-clockwise one in the next. 2004 was an anti-clockwise year and the race began in Liège in Belgium before heading south and into France. Luckily for Graham it was then due to go through the area of Northern France in which he was living. As a result, he was able to take some time off with his housemates to watch the race as it passed. The weather that day was wet, as it was during much of the early part of the race, and Graham and the group of young cyclists from different parts of Europe had to take shelter with other spectators at the side of the road. They were, however, happy to wait in their unfamiliar role of onlookers and to feel the buzz of excitement as the peloton rolled into view. It would not have been surprising if they all kept a silent thought that maybe one day they too would be part of that particular rolling procession.

July 14th is a particularly important day in French society, being Bastille Day, and the stage of the Tour that takes place then is one that demands an extra effort from all the home riders. A Bastille Day victory is extra special in the palmarès of any rider, but even more so for a Frenchman. The day, however, was particularly special for another reason, being also Graham's 21st birthday. The irony of a cyclist being born on Bastille Day would not have been lost on his team-mates and Sam (with the help of Graham's friends back in England and also of the French nation) was to make sure that it was a day to remember for them all.

Having read an article on Bradley McGee in which he recounted the story of spending his own 21st alone in France, Sam was determined that Graham would have only good memories of his own birthday. In the magazine piece, McGee had told of spending an unhappy day in which the highlight (if that is the appropriate word) was of going out by himself to celebrate with a beer and a hamburger. With his family and friends thousands of miles away, the young Australian had felt very much alone on this most significant of days. Struck by the poignancy of the image of a young bike rider alone on his birthday, Sam was determined to ensure that this did not happen to Graham. Energised by the article, she bought a large birthday card and arranged for it to be signed by Graham's family and friends. She then collected a number of presents from them, before setting off by plane to visit Graham once more in Beauvais. Once there, she enlisted the help of Dimitri and the other housemates to decorate the place with balloons for the morning of Graham's birthday. Presents and cards duly opened, Graham and Sam then spent a sunny afternoon at a local beauty spot with many other revellers. In the evening the couple went to the house of one of the team officials, where in the company of a large group they drank champagne and paid tribute (albeit unknowingly) to one of the key moments in the French Revolution of 1789. The day was rounded off with a huge midnight firework display and at its end this had been a wonderful experience for both Graham and Sam and one that they would be able to remember for the rest of their lives. Once again, this was proof, if it was needed, of the quality and diversity of the life experiences that Graham's cycling talents, Sam's initiative and the Dave Rayner Fund had made possible.

During Sam's short stay, the couple also spent a day at the Eurodisney complex outside Paris where they rode the various attractions and for a brief time the two were able to be like any other young couple, enjoying new places and meeting people from different cultures for the first time. However, it was not all play as Graham was also taking his training for the forthcoming race very seriously and when we next met it was clear that he had been successful in cutting out some of the less healthy elements from his diet.

The meeting was on the eve of the National Under-23 race and took place in the unlikely setting of the Holiday Inn, Aylesbury. The life of a cyclist involves many changes in location and over the course of the summer Julia and I had begun to experience this at first hand, with many weekends being spent away from home in the name of attending that weekend's major bike race. Again we spent Saturday on the motorway and this time we had arranged to meet Graham and Sam at the hotel some miles from the course, where we would all be staying on the night before the race.

Graham had flown into Luton from Beauvais on Friday where he was eventually met by a stressed-out Sam, who had driven down from Doncaster and in the process had been forced to negotiate a major tailback on the M1. On Friday evening the two had gone for dinner in Aylesbury and on Saturday morning they had driven the ten or so miles across to Oakley where they had done a reconnaissance of the hilly course. After driving the route, Graham had jumped on his bike and ridden a number of laps to ensure that he was fully prepared for the following day and so he knew where the attacks were most likely to come. Graham was optimistic about his chances and knew that at his best he would be one of the favourites for the title. Also, the level of groundwork that he and Sam had undertaken was indicative of the seriousness with which he was taking the event. It occurred to me that this diligent (perhaps almost perfectionist) approach seemed in stark contast to the way in which he was expected to operate in France. Perhaps, I thought, he would do well in this race because he had been left to prepare in his own thorough way rather than just being driven to a venue and told to ride. However, at the same time I knew from Tom's experiences in Belgium that the ability to race on an almost daily basis and at the drop of a hat is very much part of the elite riders job spec.

We spent early Saturday evening drinking coffee with Graham and Sam in their room, surrounded by empty bidons, assorted jerseys and shorts and various other items from the racing cyclist's kit bag, before going out together for an early meal. During this time the conversation came around to the subject of David Millar, whose story had now made the back pages of the national press and was causing a wave of upset and blood letting within the sport. Graham had met the now officially-disgraced rider at the previous year's World Championships in Canada and from his comments it seemed that my view of David Millar may have been a little overly sentimental. It was not that Graham had anything bad to say about him, just that he didn't really have anything positive to say either. According to Graham's recollections, the (soon to be ex) World Time Trial Champion had simply not been overly interested in communicating with the younger members of the team and had seemed to prefer the company of his iPod to that of other bike riders. This made me think about how we as fans lionise our sporting heroes. How it's often not enough for them to excel at what they do, but that in addition we want them to be a certain kind of person. The dreaded phrase of 'a good role model' comes to mind. But is this realistic? Sporting success demands a level of commitment to oneself that it is often at odds with acts of altruism and can at times actually demand that the individual is nothing short of selfish. Why then should we expect our sporting heroes to automatically be good guys? Having said that, I must admit to being as guilty of it as the next man.

Once back at the hotel, an anonymous building on the

outskirts of town, we had a final drink together (non-alcoholic for Graham of course) before heading off back to our rooms. Tomorrow was going to be a big day, perhaps the biggest of the season for Graham, and he and Sam were doing everything to ensure that it went well.

Sunday dawned warm and sunny. After packing our bags I came across Graham in the car park of the hotel, loading his bike into Sam's small car. Due to its high value, the carbon fibre frame and lightweight wheels had spent the previous night in Graham and Sam's room, much to the surprise of the staff, whose suggestion that he could lock it up overnight round the back of the hotel had been quietly rebuffed. We soon set off in convoy to the race Headquarters at Oakley village hall and were amongst the first to arrive. After the grand surroundings of the Celtic Manor resort this was very much a return to the small scale and low profile of cycling in Britain. However, on a positive note this is a world built on the hard work and enthusiasm of many unpaid individuals that do it simply for the love of the sport. Preferring to prepare by himself, Graham parked the car someway away from the hall. However, like all other road racers he had to then go through the ritual of signing on for the race. This is a process that involves handing over your racing licence (a small piece of plastic containing amongst other things your photograph, the name of your club and the category you have reached as a racer) and signing on the official start sheet, in exchange for a race number and a selection of safety pins with which to attach it to your jersey.

By this time a number of the other competitors had arrived, many still dressed in their everyday clothes. Naturally they began to chat amongst themselves and both Julia and I were struck by the youth of the riders. It seemed to us that the collection of skinny adolescents around us, nervously talking their own chances up or down (depending on how they chose to cope with the pressure) and gossiping about the sexual preferences of their fellow riders, couldn't possibly also be top-level athletes. However, as they began to re-emerge from the changing room some time later in their full cycling kit and as they climbed onto their racing bikes, a strange transformation seemed to occur and strangely they had become grown men. Graham looked particularly focused for the race and was not much in the mood for a pre-race laugh and joke. Instead, he had on what some sportsmen call their 'game face'.

The race rolled out of the car park and towards the hilly circuit that was to be the scene of the action that day. Sam jumped into the back of our car and we set off for the course and the point on the crest of one of the main climbs which would act as the feed station and where we would hand Graham's bottles up to him. After a period of waiting, the peloton came past for the first time and Graham, riding in the main body of the field, looked strong. From then on they came past at regular 30 minute intervals and on each occasion Graham seemed to be going well. Various attempts were made to break away, but each one was brought back, with Graham appearing to often be to the fore in the chase. As we had learned at Celtic Manor, a climb is an ideal place to feed a rider and on one or two circuits Sam was successful in passing Graham a bottle. Also, it a good position from which to pick out a particular rider from the rest of the group and from what we had seen so far, things appeared to be going to plan. After over an hour of racing the sun went in and some time later it began to rain. However, it was only a light summer drizzle and it was unlikely to inconvenience the field too much.

After a number of large laps, the race was due to move onto a small circuit and so we began to load up the supplies into the boot of the car. This was to be the last time the race would go up this particular climb and as the field came past us one last time, we prepared to offer our encouragement. But this time I didn't see Graham. Sam, Julia and I looked at each other and from our mutual expressions it was clear that none of us had noticed him. We looked for a positive though. Perhaps he'd been hidden by other riders – that can happen.

We were now beginning to worry a little. Maybe he'd had a mechanical problem and lost time. We delayed our departure just in case he was chasing to get back onto the tails of the main group. There was no sign of him though and reluctantly we climbed into the car and I began to drive up the road. I was just about to make a left turn when I glanced in the mirror and saw a figure slowly dragging himself up the climb. Surely, it couldn't be. Having made the turn I pulled the car over and after some agonising seconds Graham came around the bend, clearly in some distress. His race was over and no sooner had he seen the car than he was coming to a halt and Sam was rushing out into the rain to comfort him. For a few minutes we sat in the car as Sam consoled Graham and the scene outside was so sad that it felt as if we were intruding on other people's private grief.

We were struggling to understand how someone who had looked so strong was now so exhausted. Cycling we knew can do that to even the fittest rider, but I remembered now that Graham had previously complained of reaching points some hours into races in France when his legs would suddenly become leaden, or as he put it 'locked up'. He had no explanation for it and it was not something that he had experienced in previous years, but it appeared that the phenomenon had returned with a vengeance in this most important of races. After what we guessed was an acceptable amount of time, Julia and I climbed out of the car to offer our commiserations. Graham's first words to us were of apology and at that moment it struck me how much I had gone native. No longer was I a writer in search of story. We were fully-fledged supporters (and I hoped friends) and if truth were told, this had been the case with me from very early on. Although primarily a story of bikes and bike races, it had dawned on me that I was watching (and in a small way taking part in) pure human drama of a sort seldom accurately reproduced in fiction. As a result, I was about as far away from being the impartial chronicler of events as it was possible to be. Taking his bike and loading it into the car, we told Graham that our only concern was with his well-being, but in the moment of his disappointment it seemed a hollow sentiment. The big day, one that had begun with such high expectations, had turned decidedly sour.

Sitting in the car, with the rain falling gently on the roof, we were at a loss as to what to do next. There was after all still a race going on. After some minutes we agreed to drive back to the race HQ where Graham changed back into his civvies and now beginning to recover both physically and mentally, he told us that he wanted to go back to the circuit to see the conclusion of the race. This, I thought, although really difficult for him, was the right thing to do. A large part of him would have preferred to simply load up Sam's car and point it in the direction of South Yorkshire. However, Graham still had friends in the race and he unselfishly wanted to go back to encourage them on. One of these was the Midlands-based rider (and another recipient of the support of the Fund) Dan Fleeman.

In a sport inundated with tales of sporting tragedy and of triumph over adversity, Dan's story still managed to be outstanding. Out on a training ride in 2003, he had been involved in an accident with a car that left him with two broken kneecaps and an initial prognosis of never walking again, let alone cycling. After a long period of active convalescence, however, Dan had proved the doctors wrong. This was not enough though and he went on to take another massive leap when getting back on the bike and now here he was back to full fitness and like Graham racing and living in France.

The hilly circuit was beginning to take its toll on the field and as we took up our places on the finishing line to watch the race go past, it was clear that it had split into a number of small groups and that the winner was going to come from the first of these. The views from the top of the hill on which the race was to finish were spectacular, but the weather had now become cold and windy. The skies were dark in a way that seemed to mirror Graham's fortunes. However, each time the lead group came past Graham and Sam stood up to encourage and shout on their friends. At one point, Graham decided to walk back down the hill, where he knew one or two of the Great Britain under-23 squad were watching the race. They too had abandoned and Graham was keen to see how they had fared and also to re-establish contact with the management team. The expression on his face when he returned to us some time later suggested that things had not gone well.

Back in the race, something of a fairytale ending was in the offing. As the bell went for the start of the final lap the lead group was down to four and Dan was there. The remainder of the field came past over the following minutes before the steep road again went quiet. Although the number of spectators could be numbered in the tens there was a palpable sense of tension in the air. Then we heard them coming for the final time. We could hear cheers from down the hill and after another intense period of waiting the first rider emerged from between the hedgerows that ran along either side of the road. It was Dan and he went on to cross the line with a most ostentatious flourish, a few seconds in front of his nearest chaser. Knowing what he had been through, though, no one could deny him his moment of over-the-top celebration, or the proposal of marriage to his girlfriend that followed shortly afterwards.

What remained of the field came over the line in dribs and drabs before people gradually began to return to their cars. The presentation was to be back at the village hall and Graham and Sam decided that they wanted to go and so we joined the procession of cars that soon headed down the hill. Back at the village hall, the hardened men of the road quickly disappeared to be replaced once again by a group of adolescents. They milled around excitedly catching up on each other's experiences of the race and a number of them were genuinely surprised to learn that Graham hadn't finished. From their reactions to the news it was clear that they had seen him as a big rival.

Some then went on to ask him about his experiences in France and in a candid moment he admitted to one Scottish rider, himself living in Belgium, that he was finding things tough. The look that this brought, said much about the camaraderie and shared experience that has to exist between the Brits abroad. Without having to say much, the young man's eyes shouted, 'I know, it's hard, isn't it?'. There seemed to be genuine sympathy for Graham amongst the other riders and another suggested cheekily that he simply tell his managers back at Beauvais that he finished in the middle of the peloton, when they asked him how he had fared in the race.

Graham then went back to talk to the Great Britain under-23 squad who were by now larking about and telling horror stories of their experiences living together in rented houses in one of the main student areas of Manchester. This time though he also had a serious purpose. Having had some time to digest the events of the day, Graham and Sam were keen to explore the reasons for his recent inability to complete races. It didn't appear to be down to a lack of fitness and so maybe there was a medical reason. How, though, would he be able to find out? It was unlikely that he would get much help in Beauvais. Their answer to all ills appeared in France to be to train harder and to eat less. Perhaps instead the Great Britain set-up would be willing to let Graham use their extensive medical facilities. Maybe the team doctor could do a blood test for Graham. He had after all represented his country on more than one occasion during the season. Graham asked one of the other members of the squad, whom he knew had recently been ill with a viral infection, whether he thought it would be a good idea to ask. However, at that very moment one of the team officials came past, and with a quick put-down of that rider, unequivocally ruled out the possibility. Graham was on his own, and the fickle nature of sporting fortune was once more set out in stark relief. Now that he wasn't winning, it seemed that no one wanted to know.

Shortly afterwards the presentation began and this served as a welcome diversion from the unhappy events of the day. Dan Fleeman took his place on the top of a homemade podium and pulled on the national champion's jersey to spirited applause and then the second and third placed riders (Richard Whitehorn and Ben Greenwood) were presented with their prizes. To add to the sense of improvisation, Dan was handed a small bunch of flowers before being asked questions over a faulty PA system. As the interview ended Dan went off to answer more questions from a journalist and the crowd began to disperse. Observing as the protagonists began to leave the scene, there was already a clutch of fully-fledged images circulating in my mind. There was drama, Graham's heartbreak and for Dan the moment of pure ecstasy as he crossed the line as a winner. There were also the little things though, such as the lightness of Graham's bike as I placed it in the car after he had abandoned and also his unused bidons, still full of their thick energy drink. Each told a story of its own.

We said our final goodbyes to Sam and Graham and began to walk back to the car in readiness for the Sunday night drive north. Graham was heading back to Doncaster for another week at home and this time he had some serious thinking to do. It was now highly unlikely that he would be selected for the Great Britain team for the European championships in August and his place at the Worlds was also in jeopardy. At the same time, these concerns were now almost secondary to the need to get to the bottom of the problem that had forced him to abandon the day's race. A season that had started so brightly was now in danger of falling apart and for almost the first time since he had taken up the sport of cycling, Graham was experiencing what it was like to suffer. To make it worse, he didn't know the cause. I thought back to the sense of frustration I felt when I fell ill and went from doctor to doctor who were unable to tell me what was wrong. It brought a shudder to my spine and I could only hope that his family and friends would be there for him and would help get him through this newly arrived crisis.

CHAPTER 10

Friday the Thirteenth

AS JULY BECAME August our thoughts moved toward our annual holiday in Normandy. Julia being a teacher was to spend three weeks in Barneville-Carteret, whilst I (having a proper job) was looking forward to joining her for the final two of those weeks. The holiday, however, also provided me with the opportunity to pay further visits to Tom and Graham and also to catch up with Cheeky Phil Evans who lived only an hour's drive from where we would be staying.

In the aftermath of the Under-23 road race, Graham had returned home to lick his wounds and to seek medical advice. With no support forthcoming from British Cycling, he was in need of help and was lucky enough to be put in contact with a GP in the Doncaster area who himself was a keen cyclist. The doctor, although not a specialist in sports medicine, had offered to give Graham a blood test and to analyse the results for him. This though would take time and Graham took the decision to stay in the UK and to rest until he had received the results. This meant that as I flew out to Paris (before taking a Friday evening train bound for Cherbourg) we were in the unusual situation that I was heading to France, but Graham was in the UK. This irony particularly struck home as the train made an early stop in the town of Evreux, the site of Graham's big early season win.

After a few days relaxing with Julia and settling into the wonderfully slow pace of our holiday, I began to make calls to arrange my range of meetings. Graham's French mobile was dead and from that I judged that he was still resting at home. Tom, on the other hand was very much in action, enjoying a diet of important post Tour de France one-day races and Belgian Kermesses. In fact the day before we talked, he had been in a race in Germany in which he had spent most of the time in a group that included the Italian Ivan Basso (who had just finished in third place in the Tour de France) and the renowned German sprinter Erich Zabel – exalted company indeed. We agreed that Julia and I would travel up to Belgium on Thursday 12th August before watching Tom ride a professional Kermesse in the small town of Buggenhout on the following day. This was to be a bread and butter event for Tom and I was keen to experience at close hand one of his typical days at work.

We set off early on Thursday to make the long drive north to our overnight stop in Mons, just over the border in the French-speaking part of Belgium. Our route took us past Amiens and near to Beauvais. Amiens is an attractive city with a beautiful cathedral and the journey brought back more memories of the previous year, when I had cycled through the region. I was pleased to think that this was a part of the world that I was now beginning to know well, but with Graham back in Doncaster there was little reason for us to stop. We passed into Belgium late in the afternoon and finally drew into Mons (a town with great significance for historians like Julia and myself, due to the role it played in the First World War) around 6pm. We checked into our hotel and in the early evening sunshine began to walk towards the town's main square where we looked forward to eating dinner. However, as we neared the centre of town we were engulfed in a massive thunderstorm. August 2004 seemed to be characterised by such storms throughout Western Europe and dressed as we were for a summer evening, there was little to expect but a severe drenching. In fact, so hard was the rain that the roads quickly became flooded and to a couple of unprotected tourists like ourselves, it was like being in the firing line of water cannon. Eventually the rain relented enough to allow us to make a run for it. Disconsolately, we trudged back to the hotel where we changed, showered and went to eat in its own restaurant. So much for Mons.

We were up early on Friday to complete our journey to the eastern suburbs of Brussels. There was more rain that morning, but our journey was uneventful. That was until a point at which all the road signs suddenly seemed to change. From knowing where we were, it appeared that we were now heading towards a totally different set of towns. We wondered what was going on. It was only after some time that we realised that we were now in the Flemish-speaking part of Belgium and all the place names were now in a different language.

After around ninety minutes driving we found ourselves on the Brussels ring road heading towards Tervuren. A short time later we pulled up in the town itself and it was at this point that I remembered that I had not previously visited Roger's house. In addition, at that point we didn't actually have anywhere to stay that night. Somewhat surprisingly Tervuren's one hotel (the one that I had stayed in at Easter) was fully booked and so after making more phone calls we found ourselves a room in the town of Leuven, some 15 miles or so to the east. With our accommodation sorted, I rang Tom to be given directions to the house and after a few more minutes of driving around we found ourselves next to his car, the unmistakable Silver Bird. This had to be it and sure enough Tom quickly emerged from the house to welcome us and to offer us coffee.

We went inside to be met by Liv, who after catching a ridiculously cheap but early flight from England was at the start of a week-long visit. The couple had met in Leeds, where Liv been a student, over the previous winter, but they had been forced to conduct a long distance relationship for most of their time together. Now though they could look forward to some quality time – that was of course when Tom wasn't racing or training or hosting visits from writers and their partners. Roger was not at home at the time of our visit, having a prior engagement with a small event known as the Olympic Games. In fact, Roger was to ride the Men's Road Race in Athens only twenty-four hours later on Saturday morning.

Roger's house, although large, lacked a certain feminine

touch. Radiators were covered in drying cycling kit and everywhere there were items of bike-riding ephemera. This was not surprising, as the three inhabitants of the property were all full-time cyclists. Tom claimed that an Australian woman who worked as a soigneur for a professional team lived in a small house in the garden, but we saw no evidence to substantiate the rumour. In one of the few concessions to home comforts one wall had a photograph of a young Roger winning the World Junior Cyclo-Cross championship at Roundhay Park in Leeds.

Shortly before our arrival, news had begun to emerge that Roger was to leave his current Belgian team, Mr.Book maker.com, to transfer across to Lance Armstrong's US Postal team, which in turn was to be re-named after its new sponsors, the Discovery Channel. Tom confirmed that this indeed was likely and I asked him how it would affect own his chances of gaining a stagiare contract with the Mr.Bookmaker.com team. Tom was honest enough to accept that although great news for Roger, the move could have a negative impact on his own aspirations. With his imminent departure from the team, Roger's influence over the managers of the Mr.Bookmaker.com team would be on the wane and so Tom's links to Roger would no longer be a positive. This impression was further reinforced when Tom told me that another young British rider, Yanto Barker, had made the trip north from his summer base in France to ride a few August races in Belgium and that he was staying with Jez Hunt. It was likely that Jez would be putting a good word in for Yanto in the way that Roger would have done for Tom.

It was late morning by the time of our arrival and after catching up on these recent events and on the state of the sport back home, Tom began to prepare for the race. The race was not an official team event and so he had to make his own arrangements. A few cups of strong coffee and a rudimentary home-made energy drink were prepared and quaffed before he began to arrange his kit. The bike was retrieved from the garage and it and a collection of wheels were placed in the boot of the car. It wasn't exactly haphazard, but Tom's pre-race routine certainly had the air of the everyday to it.

Deciding to travel to the race in one car, we jumped into the Silver Bird for the forty-minute drive to Buggenhout, scene that day of the 23rd Grote Prijs Jozef Van Der Jeugt. Buggenhout is only a small town and soon after leaving the motorway we became lost. This was now a familiar feeling to me: driving at high speed down country roads in the hope (more than expectation) of finding a race HQ. The situation was not improved by the lack of road signs in that part of the world. It was as if everyone that travelled the back roads of Belgium was expected to already know where they were going. A few unexplained road closures and intermittent rainstorms only added to the sense of chaos and tension and at one point Tom was in serious danger of failing to even find the race, let alone take part in it. We were in the midst of putting our ill luck down to the curse of Friday 13th, but fortunately we began to come upon a succession of elderly cyclists that we guessed were on their way to watch the race. After stopping and asking directions in Flemish from one of these, Tom became more confident of the way to the start and the speed in the car began to increase as a consequence.

Eventually we pulled up on the main street of Buggenhout and Tom jumped out of the car to run to the HQ to sign on. It seemed a good idea for me to put the bike together whilst Tom was away, and so making an executive decision I took the two most likely looking wheels and slipped them into place before tightening the quick release skewers. At this point Tom returned with his race number to inform me that I had managed to pick out and fit his spares, whilst his best wheels remained in the boot of the car. After a quick change the bike was now ready, but Tom was still in his everyday clothes. The skies were growing dark again at this point and not having time to be embarrassed he began to change into his cycling kit under the cover of a carport of a nearby house. He then climbed on his bike and set off for the start and the next time we saw him, we has in the main body of the field at it headed towards us down the street. He had made it, but only just.

As the field disappeared into the distance on the first of the twelve laps that made up the 166km race distance, Julia, Liv and

I decided to have a look around to see what sights Buggenhout had to offer. This did not take long and with a main thoroughfare called Krapstraat, it was no great surprise that there was little to grab the attention apart from a selection of bars and a fast-food outlet. On one corner, however, was a bookie, who had a board containing the names of the fancied riders in the race and their odds to win. Sitting there at around 25 to 1 was Hamish Haynes and we thought he could be a good outside bet. In the end we decided to save our Euros and this proved to be a good decision as Hamish lasted only a few laps before abandoning.

Manning an ancient PA system by the start–finish line was the middle-aged race announcer who kept the crowd up to date with progress as the race went into the country lanes around the town. Obviously this was in Flemish and so we were not able to keep up to speed with the breaks. However, in between updates the MC delighted in playing a selection of soporific tunes from the 1950s and 60s. I lost count of the number of times that we were serenaded that day with the awful 'Tell Laura I Love Her' and all through a sound system that seemed to possess no bass tones whatsoever. As the record came on once again, I wondered what the suicide rate must be in this part of Belgium.

After stopping to eat (a memorable experience for those of us who had never tasted fried chicken burger topped with coronation chicken mayonnaise) we bought a race programme and Liv, who was feeling the effects of her early start to the day, went back to the car to sleep. Looking through the race line-up, I managed to count some six Brits in the field of around 100, as well as seven Australians. By this time we had a distinct sense of being stared at. It said much for the life of the inhabitants of Buggenhout that we were what passed for exotic. Tom was to tell us later that this was common and without being prejudiced, Belgians were known for staring. Liv's experience as she tried to sleep in the car, however, was not helped by the fact that Tom had left a large sign reading 'Please Pay Here' (taken from a pie shop in England) on the dashboard of the Silver Bird.

The course was flat and although the road surface was not good, the race was staying together. However, the pace at the front was punishingly fast and each lap brought its fresh batch of retirees. One such was Alex Coutts, a young Scottish rider of the Dave Rayner Fund, and one of those that had shown sympathy towards Graham at the under-23 road race at Oakley. Having seem him confidently climb the hills of South Wales and Buckinghamshire it struck me that the flatlands of Belgium may not be the best location for a rider with talents such as his. Eventually, a small group rode away from the rest of the field and they went on to contest the finish. However, when the Belgian winner made his decisive move to cross the line alone, the large crowd that had now gathered responded with little more than silence. It was clear that he was not a local favourite and indeed it was a little surprising that he was not followed over the line by a ball of tumbleweed, such was the under whelming nature of the response to his victory.

Tom, as ever, rode to the end and finished in the main group, but the end of the race brought little in the way of ceremony. After crossing the line the riders simply rode back to their cars and began to put their bikes away. A few stayed around for a chat, but as it was threatening to rain once again and as there were no showers at the HQ, many just headed straight for home. On this occasion we didn't stay to watch the presentation, but Tom's description of a typical after-race prizegiving left us content that we had not missed much. Often, he said, the winning riders had to brave the smoke-fuelled atmosphere of the local bar, pushing past the punters on the way, to retrieve their not inconsiderable prize money. It didn't sound like the best kind of warm-down for someone who has just ridden 100 miles in the rain.

Soon we were back in the car and making our way back to Tervuren. On the return journey we passed another bike race and at another juncture found ourselves in a small town that was in the process of being cordoned off for a race on the following day. With some excellent driving skills Tom managed to negotiate the town in one piece and it really seemed true what he had told me about being able to take part in a race on any day of the week in Belgium during the summer. Once back at the house, we met Matt as he prepared his evening meal. He had been out training when we arrived earlier in the day and was now getting ready to tuck into the eminently healthy meal of chicken and broccoli before spending an evening in front of the TV. Turning down our offer of a free feed, Matt stayed at home whilst the four of us went to 'the' Tervuren pizza restaurant. This was now the third time I had eaten there, but from the looks on the faces of the owners as we entered, Tom was now a much more regular visitor. We spent the next couple of hours reflecting on the day and also gaining some funny and interesting insights from Liv into the eccentricities of the cycling fraternity as witnessed by someone with no background in the sport. There was the time, for example, when she entered Tom's parents home in Yorkshire to find him stretched out on the kitchen table receiving a massage from his Dad. The scene was only topped by the fact that when Tom had finished, Jez, who was staying with them at the time, then jumped up on the table to take his turn.

Eventually, we realised that it was getting late and we still had to drive to Leuven for our overnight stay. Thanking both Tom and Liv for a great day, we headed back to our car. Tom wished us a safe journey before adding that there was a free rock festival going on over the weekend in Leuven and if we wanted to, we might see some well-known bands. Finally, he invited us back to Roger's to watch his landlord take part in the Olympic Road Race the following morning. What a great offer – to watch the British Champion race in the Olympics from his own front room.

It had begun to rain heavily by this point and Julia drove carefully until we reached the outskirts of the town. It looked as though we had emerged unscathed from the curse of Friday the Thirteenth, but as we approached the centre we became aware that a number of the roads were barricaded off. Perhaps they've closed some off for the concert, we thought, not realising that the entire town centre was cordoned off from traffic. Some fifty minutes later we were still trying to find our way into the historic centre of the town, with its medieval cathedral, and more importantly with our hotel in it. Things by this stage were getting tense in the car and I decided that the only way to find the hotel was on foot. We parked up the car and I set off into town in the rain. In a few minutes I was surrounded by thousands of drunken Belgians wigging out to bad Euro-rock. To make things somehow worse, although the majority of their conversations were held in Flemish, they cursed in English. Such was my grim mood by this point that a few people were lucky not to learn some new words of Anglo-Saxon, as I made my way through the thick crowds. Eventually I found the hotel, barely 100 yards from one of the numerous stages. Then it was back to the car, which at first I couldn't find. More heated words followed when I did finally return, before we decided to leave the car and to make our way to the hotel on foot. The rain was now heavier than ever and the people even more drunk. It was like a walk into hell, a perception that was only intensified when we finally made it into our room, to find that the thermostat was broken and we couldn't lower the temperature. The alternative was to open the window and be subjected to more of the Michael Schenker Group, or the Scorpions, or whichever Germanic Monster of Rock was playing a selection of its greatest hits directly into the room. It was around three in the morning when things began to quieten down outside. We were now finally drifting off to sleep and I remember my final words that night – Friday the Fucking Thirteenth!

I woke on Saturday morning to find Julia gone. Had it been that bad? However, before I could panic she was knocking on the door of the room. In an act of supreme decisiveness she had got up early, found the car and moved it to a spot just around the corner from the hotel. The plan (which was not up for discussion) was to eat breakfast before heading back to France (and civilization) as quickly as possible. After the night we had endured I couldn't argue, even if it did mean missing Roger in the Olympics. We spent Saturday driving back to Barneville-Carteret whilst Roger, cheered on by Tom, Liv and Matt back in Belgium (and a few million more on worldwide TV) finished a fantastic seventh in the race.

We spent the following couple of days recuperating by the sea and it took little more than one or two strolls along the beautiful beach and a couple of glasses of locally-produced cider to rid us of the after effects of Friday 13th. However, I still wanted to find out if Graham was in France and in addition I was waiting to hear from Cheeky Phil to see if he would have the time to meet us in the final week of our holiday. Although I tried the number time and again, there was still no answer on Graham's French mobile. If appearances were true, he had been back in England now for around three weeks and I was beginning to worry that he had been diagnosed with some medical complaint, or that he had decided simply not to come back to France to finish the season. At the same time I did not want to ring him in England for fear of adding to the pressures that he might be under at the time. In the end I decided to let things lie for a while.

In any case, I had now received a call from Phil saying that although he was very busy, he would be able to meet us during his lunch break from the Decathlon sports store where he worked. This was an added bonus and we set off excitedly on Thursday morning to travel down the Cotentin Peninsula to the border of Normandy and Brittany, and the coastal town of Avranche. Driving down it dawned on me that despite our shared history I had only ever properly met Phil once and that there was more than a little of the surreal about our friendship. It even occurred to me that I might not recognise him, but in the end it was easy to spot Phil as we entered the store. He was the one hanging around the entrance to the store with a cassette from the back wheel of a bike in his hand. We drove back into the centre of Avranche from the retail park on which the Decathlon was sited and Phil took us to a café that he visited regularly. As we entered this particular eaterie it was again clear that this was a valued customer.

Going it alone and working full time to pay his way had affected Phil's riding during 2004 and he admitted that the adjustment had not been easy. In fact his season had already petered out and he wasn't racing a great deal by this point. However, away from cycling life was good and he told us that his parents were going to buy a place nearby in anticipation of retiring to France. In the meantime, Phil and his French girlfriend would be able to live in the house.

After ordering lunch in fluent French, Phil went on to tell us that there was a road race organised by his club in Briquebec on the following Sunday and that although not in great form, he would be taking part. In addition, Phil thought it highly likely that Graham's Beauvais team would also be taking part. I couldn't believe that we didn't know this and it left us with some decision-making to do as we were due to catch the ferry home on the day before the race. The prospect of watching the race go up the steep, cobbled main street in the town and past the old castle was a mouth watering one and we were sorely tempted to stay an extra day. At the same time it made it all the more important to find out if Graham was indeed in France or still at home. We agreed to keep in touch with Phil and told him that there was a chance that we would be at the race on Sunday, but only if we could re-schedule our travelling arrangements. Our time with Phil was over all too quickly and it was soon time for him to go back to work. However, this was not before he had caught up on all aspects of gossip concerning his old mates at ABC Centreville. Such was his inquisitiveness that after the meeting Julia too had no need to ask, Why Cheeky Phil?

Although lasting no longer than 2 hours, our meeting with Phil had a deep effect on us. It was wonderful to think that the Dave Rayner Fund had helped to shape this young man's life in such a way as to change his horizons forever and also that the ripples of his decision to go to France were still being felt, even among his family back in England. At the same time, it seemed like our relationship with Normandy was in some way validated by seeing Phil and also that it now sat in a changed context, knowing that there was a growing number of people from our part of the world that had grown to love it too. The skies were once again slate grey for most of the journey north to Barneville-Carteret, but inside our hearts had a sunny glow.

Over the next days I tried Graham's mobile on more than one occasion, but there was still no sign that he was in France and so reluctantly we decided to stick by our original travel arrangements. On Saturday 21st August we caught the fast ferry from Cherbourg to Poole and made our way home. This was the fourth consecutive year that we had visited our beloved

Barneville. However, this visit was different from previous ones, in that as well as a holiday it was an opportunity to meet friends. The fact that this involved over two day's driving was a mere detail. This was a wonderful feeling and one that not even the curse of Friday the Thirteenth could spoil.

CHAPTER 11

Homeward Bound

OUR HOLIDAY OVER, we returned to England and once again I attempted to contact Graham. This time, though, I was successful. A phone call established that he was indeed at home in Doncaster and had been so since that bad day at Oakley. He was , however, also planning to go back to France for the last month of the season. Early in the year his plan had been to be in the UK in early September, to defend his Under-23 time-trial title and to compete in the Tour of the Peak, one day Premier Calendar race. The way in which events unfolded, though, meant that this was no longer possible.

The time-trial had been one of Graham's big wins of the previous year and had been something of a surprise as it was not a discipline he specialised in. It would have been good to return as the defending champion, but the uncertainties over his health led in turn to delays in sending off his entry form and in the end he missed the deadline for the race. Even as the titleholder no exceptions were to be made and so the opportunity to race in the UK as a reigning champion was lost. At the same time, the Tour of the Peak was cancelled due to a clash of dates with the newly re-instated Tour of Britain. As well as the disappointment for Graham I was also left to rue the changing situation. I had long looked forward to simply going out on the bike with Tom or Graham and I had arranged with Graham to go for a ride together during what remained of his time at home. To simply potter around the lanes of Lancashire or Yorkshire chatting and sharing our common passion for the bike would have been the icing on the cake for me and so I was regretful that Graham had to make this late change of plan.

As far as his health was concerned, the blood tests had not found any abnormalities and he was no nearer an explanation for the problems he had been having. After a period of total rest and having experienced some home comforts though, he was now feeling much better in himself. In fact, he had even taken part in a race in Yorkshire over a recent weekend. Looking back, we can only conjecture as to the reasons for Graham's fatigue, but it is possible that it had its roots in the sheer amount of training and racing that he was asked to do in 2004. This was far in excess of anything that he had done previously and perhaps his body was just not ready for the additional stresses and strains of his first year as a full-time bike rider.

Whatever Graham's reasons were, I was cheered to find that he was intending to go back to Beauvais. As time had gone on it had worried me that he would choose to draw a line under his French adventure, and remaining in England for the last part of the season must have been a tempting prospect. However, he knew that this would not do his career prospects any good. The Fund would be less likely to continue to support him and the chances of either staying with UC Beauvais, or of finding another club would not be helped if a perception existed that he had not stayed the course. A return to France, no matter how brief, was the right course of action and one that was going to stand him in better stead going forward.

So Graham went back to France and a short time afterwards a major stage race came back to home shores. After a number of years without such an event, the return of the Tour of Britain had been announced earlier in 2004. Excitement in the cycling fraternity grew later in the year as the route and the list of competing teams was announced. It was here that serendipity again took a hold. Stage one was a large loop starting and finishing in Manchester, and taking in large swathes of Lancashire. In a tremendous piece of luck, the race would even pass by our very front door, before heading up the short but fearsome climb of the Ramsbottom Rake. Also, among the major professional teams taking part was Roger and Jez's Mr.Bookmaker.com outfit.

The race began on the 1st of September, which proved to be a warm late summer day. The crowds on the hill that morning were large and having been dissuaded by Julia from getting out the emulsion and painting names on the road the night before (à la the Tour de France) I was determined to give the riders a hearty cheer as they came past. The Rake came early in the day and they were still fresh as they attempted to climb the hill. As a result, whilst there was the opportunity to see some of the world's top pro's it was simply too early on in the day for them to be struggling (or 'creeping' as Tom's circle called it). Consequently, there were few alarms before the field moved off towards Pendle Hill. From there, the route took them west where eventually the peloton rolled along the promenade at Blackpool, with the gaudy splendour of the Golden Mile as a backdrop, before turning back towards Manchester. I wondered what the riders would have made of the famous sights of this unique seaside town as they passed the Tower, the three piers and the Pleasure Beach.

Inspired by the crowds and the weather, Toni (who had come up to watch the race with us) and I decided to go out on our bikes and we caught the race later in the day as it came back through Belmont on the outskirts of Bolton. What a glorious day it was. Top-level bike racing in the sun and on one's own doorstep. The final run into Manchester was not without its traffic problems that day (the race employed a rolling road-block rather than closing roads for hours before and after the race passed by) and on a number of occasions the peloton found itself in the middle of heavy traffic. This showed that there were a few teething troubles to overcome, but they were ironed out over the course of the week and by the time the race ended on Sunday (in a criterium race around Westminster), it had gone very well and had gained some great coverage for the sport.

Back in France, Graham was doing his best to get through the final month of his season. His cause was not helped by the temporary loss of his race bike during the transit to Beauvais, meaning that he had to sit out a few late season races. Eventually it was located and returned to him by embarrassed airport staff. In Belgium, however, Tom was still performing at a creditable level on a daily basis. In one professional Kermesse, he rode off early in the day down the road in a lone attack. Later joined by a group of other riders he stayed in the leading group throughout the race in what was an eye-catching performance. Although he was pipped for victory (the race going to one of Tom's own team-mates) his was very much the ride of the day. To be going so strongly in September, some eight months into the season, demanded great amounts of both physical and mental fortitude.

This is the time of year when riders' thoughts turn to where they will be plying their trade in the following season. The grapevine is particularly active and the rumours abound of riders moving to this or that team and one move can easily initiate a domino effect thereby presenting opportunities to other riders. Tom was at a crossroads in his career. At 24 he was unlikely to receive support from the Fund in 2005 and so had to either find a way of making cycling pay or reconcile himself to getting himself a job alongside his sporting career. This might also entail a return to Britain, but he was reluctant to go back to what he had grown to see as an inferior level of racing. Such an attitude was understandable from someone who had enjoyed over three years racing on the continent, and it was one that had been reinforced by his experiences when he rode the Grainger with Roger and Jez. There they were able to dominate proceedings without much difficulty and although it made him some money, it did not inspire him.

At this point Tom had a number of potential offers brewing, including one from Cyclingnews.com. In truth, he thought that a change of scene might be good, but the team was looking to run with a larger budget in 2005 and as a result would possibly be able to pay its riders more than just the expenses that they received in 2004. Tom, with his experience, could become a key player in the team. Ideally, however, he was looking to move to a division two team, where the money and prospects would be even better, as Tom's team-mate Hilton Clarke had done, by joining the US-based Navigators team.

Graham too, was considering moving on. After his wonderful start to the season, his experience at Beauvais had not ultimately been a positive one. He had learned a lot, but not in a particularly encouraging environment. Having a thick skin seems to be one of the key elements of many a cyclist's make-up and although Graham had started to develop this over the year, he was now ready for a more professionally run and supportive outfit. He favoured a move to another amateur club in France or Belgium. However, he was particularly keen to join a club that already had English-speaking talent in its ranks and to this end he had spoken to one or two of the riders that he had competed against at the under-23 road race in July. Meanwhile, back home in the UK, Sam was also keeping an ear to the ground regarding any opportunities that might arise closer to home.

It was also looking clear by this point that Graham would not be going to the World Championships in Verona at the start of October – at least not as a competitor – the chosen riders for the under-23 (or Espoirs) race being Keiran Page, Dan Fleeman and Evan Oliphant. However, he was still keen to be in Verona as a spectator and a party of around fifteen, including Sam and many of his best friends in the sport, was already booked to set off from Doncaster for the weekend.

With October looming, Tom in his own words finally 'cracked'. After a long year of racing, both his physical and mental resources had finally been exhausted and he sat out the last few days of his time in Belgium. He seemed in some ways disappointed at not making it to the final race of the season, but I thought it entirely understandable. It had been a long, tough but productive year. Perhaps it did not contain the one or two outstanding and career forging performances that he would have liked, but it had been more than solid and very consistent. It would be a season that he would be able to look back on with pride. After a few day's recuperation he began to gather his belongings in readiness for returning to the UK. At the same time Tom's Australian team-mates were also booking their flights home, with a significant difference though, in that they were heading back to the summer and more racing. To me this seemed like a double-edged sword. The warmth of the southern sun would be most welcome as autumn set in around Europe. However, would they really benefit from flogging their already tired bodies even more? With the Silver Bird loaded up Tom drove to a Channel ferry port and on to England. Another year of competition was over and he had to now concern himself with earning some money over the winter

Graham too, headed back at the end of September, but his initial stay back in Doncaster was a short one. He had managed to find himself a hastily-arranged place on the Verona trip and Graham, Sam and the others spent a long weekend in the beautiful Italian city, watching three races including the under-23 road race. This must have been an unusual experience for him. In 2003 he had been part of the field and from early in the season he had openly harboured ambitions of gaining selection once more. Also, both Caspar and Dimitri were involved, representing their respective nations of Estonia and Moldova and all the British team were very well known to him. In the end none of the Brits managed to complete the race and although the hilly course would not have suited Graham's sprinting talents, the results must have left him with feelings of what might have been. Sunday brought the men's elite race and Graham and Sam were again among the large crowds that thronged the course. After watching the Spaniard Oscar Freire take the world title, the Doncaster party made a quick dash to their hotel and on to the airport for a Sunday evening flight back home.

Both Tom and Graham were back in the UK and in out-of-season mode by the time of the Rayner's ride on Sunday 10th October. Tom was working full-time for the Keighley-based internet bike shop, Xpedia.com and Graham was also working, in his case delivering TV licenses in the Doncaster area. Both were having spells off the bike before they began to prepare for the following season. However, the Ride brought them out one more time. In the week before, I spoke to Graham and we agreed to meet in the town square at Skipton and to do the Ride together. At last I would get my chance to cycle with one of these two talented young men. At the same time, I sent a number of emails to Tom to see if he would like to do the same. These were not answered, but when I arrived on the day he was there, standing next to the family motorhome, which was today being used as the HQ for the Ride. Graham was also there, with Sam, and she was going to do the shorter 30 mile version of the rolling route, through the Yorkshire dales.

It was nice to catch up with all three once more and after I had enquired about the usual range of career-related subjects it was time to set off. Tom was also going to do the shorter route, but on a tandem with his younger brother. I was a little apprehensive at the prospect of riding with Graham and wondered if I would be able to keep up. The Ride was led off by the well-known cycling broadcaster Phil Liggett and soon hundreds of cyclists were heading into the country lanes around Skipton. After a few miles we found ourselves on the road in a group with Dudley Hayton. Dudley enquired how Graham's season had gone and he proudly told him of his victory in Paris–Evreux. Dudley then told us of the plans to revamp the Ride for 2005, plans which involved a move to an earlier and warmer time of year and a longer and tougher route.

Many of those taking part in the Ride were local club members and at the front things were fairly competitive. In fact for some this was the final race of the season. Having enjoyed a chat with Dudley and one or two others, Graham and I were a little way off the front group and so he decided to up the pace to make it across. For a while it looked like my worst fears were to be realised as I struggled to keep on Graham's wheel. Despite being nowhere near his top form, Graham was still strong and I was breathing heavily as the front group came into sight and was in the process of finally losing his wheel when salvation came in the form of a slow-moving bus that was between us and the leaders. The road was narrow and twisting and so each time the bus came to a stop so did we. By the time we managed to negotiate our way around it the leading group was long gone. I was secretly relieved at the turn of events, as I didn't want my one and only ride with Graham to turn into an exhausting humiliation. The challenge of the unofficial race now over the pace slowed, and we continued on with another group of riders that had already become detached. This continued for the remainder of the fifty plus miles of the Ride. At one point, the route takes in a loop around some of the most picturesque villages in England and we were surprised to see the leading group coming back towards us. Looking at the expressions of the riders it was clear to us that the race was well and truly on and inside I said a little thank you to the obstructive bus driver. After some three hours or so in the saddle we came into Gargrave. I was still in one piece and felt proud to be completing the ride in the company of a 'proper' cyclist.

The Fund had organised refreshments in the village hall and as we rolled in Tom, who had finished his route around an hour earlier, was making his preparations to ride the heavy-looking tandem back home to Keighley. It struck me that here was someone equally at home in the professional peloton and on the front of a tandem with his kid brother on a cold October morning. Again I was aware that here was a man of substance. Although it is a distinctly uncool quality to possess, Tom was and is inherently decent. Inside the hall we caught up with Sam who had been waiting patiently for Graham and I to return. With coffee and sandwiches in hand I talked to them both about the season that had just come to an end. We agreed that although the early victory had been great, it had also become an albatross around Graham's neck. Nevertheless, his commitment to the sport seemed to glow as strongly as ever and Sam too was still committed to the cause. As with Tom, the dream lived on.

Graham had learnt a lot during the year and he was determined to go back in 2005 and put these lessons into practice. Chief among these was to temper his winter training a little more and to try to peak in the middle of the year rather than at the start. It was clear that Graham had hit the season in prime fitness and that this had played a part in his victory. However, it was nigh on impossible to maintain these levels over the course of the summer, and as he now realised, his form had been tailing off at precisely the same time as his rivals had been hitting their straps. As a result, he needed to take things a little easier over the winter and so had decided that he wouldn't be going out training so much with Kev Dawson and John Tanner, his mentors from the previous year. He had now also made a formal arrangement with a coach who would guide him through his off-season

At this point I bumped into Dudley once more and he asked me how the project was coming along. As we talked, I could tell that he was particularly interested in how I had handled the tricky subject of drugs. David Millar, of course had been a Fund rider (albeit only for one year). Dudley obviously didn't want the reputation of the Fund to suffer the stigma of guilt by association and I sensed that in some ways he would have liked me to have omitted that particular thread from the overall story. As I had come to understand, the Fund is important to a great many people. It was born out or tragedy and love and its image was not to be treated lightly. All I could say to him is that I had tried and would continue to be honest in my treatment of the issue. Denial would simply not be a credible response, but I was at pains to stress that my experiences of the cycling fraternity had been overwhelmingly positive.

Dudley then took the opportunity to introduce me to John and Barbara Rayner, Dave's Mum and Dad, who were there with Dave's brother Gary. This was a moment that I had long prepared myself for, but I was still very nervous. In some ways the whole year had felt like one long job interview. One in which I had to prove the validity of my intentions, as well as my skills as a writer, to an never-ending list of people. This was now the final selection panel – or so I wrongly thought. Both were friendly and seemed genuinely interested in the project and in Tom and Graham in particular. In hindsight it was no surprise that John and Barbara were solid, kind and down to earth. These were qualities that I had often heard mentioned in relation to their son. It certainly helped keep me on an even keel, as I once more explained the journey that we had made together. I was simply thankful to be put at ease in these circumstances – it meant a lot.

After a brief presentation hosted by Tom's Dad and a call for us all to look out for Phil Liggett, who was still somewhere on the local roads, it was time to leave. I loaded my bike into the car and set off for home. Today had seen another set of significant milestones – a bike ride with Graham and a meeting with the parents of the man who gave his name to the Fund. Driving home on that cold grey afternoon, it struck me hard that my journey was nearly over. For Tom and Graham this was merely a quiet time in the year before the big push for the next season, but for me it was the beginning of the end. Soon I would no longer be sending emails and text messages and making regular phone calls to my two subjects. I had learned and experienced so much during the year and most importantly I had been genuinely lucky to meet so many warm and wonderful people. At the same time I had brushed against some of the biggest stories in the sport. Many of these had been positive, but inevitably one or two had shone a light on the murkier elements of cycling. Looking ahead, 2005 was looking like a fairly dull prospect after all the adventures of the current year.

Looking at things from another perspective, I was also sure that the conclusion of the journey would be something of a mixed blessing for Tom and Graham. On occasion my attentions must have been a chore and an intrusion and there would have been times when they would have welcomed a break from my persistent curiosity. However, at the same time, as Julia pointed out, what young sportsman would not like to be the subject of a book? Both their careers and sense of pride stood to benefit in such circumstances. I just hoped that the good had outweighed the bad.

As I neared Ramsbottom I said to myself with no little sadness that our season in the sun was now over. I reached home, cleaned my summer racing bike one last time and put it in pride of place in the dining room where it would stay for the winter. However, I wasn't quite ready for it all to end and an unexpected phone call from Dudley was to give me the perfect opportunity to go out in style.

CHAPTER 12

The Last Waltz

OCTOBER GAVE WAY to November. Cyclists of all levels were spending spend more time indoors and some were even taking a complete break from riding the bike. Tom, for example, was now doing sessions at the gym, designed to rebuild some of the muscle mass he had lost over the gruelling summer months. It had only been weeks, but already the previous season, with all its highs and lows, seemed a long way away.

I was idly watching television one dark cold night, with cycling far from my mind, when the phone rang. I was surprised that it was Dudley and he was ringing to let me know that he had come into possession of a spare ticket for the forthcoming Dave Rayner Fund annual dinner. As I knew, the dinner was one of the biggest events in the social calendar and tickets had been in short supply all year. Luckily for me, one of Dudley's own party had cancelled and so I had the offer of a seat on one of the best tables in the house. I felt touched that he had thought of me, as the list of frustrated potential attendees was a long one. Also, I had long since given up hope of attending, and so the factor of surprise only added to my glee as I put down the telephone and passed on the news to Julia. To add to the excitement, both Tom and Graham would be there and the guest of honour at the event was to be none other than the great Eddy Merckx.

Over the following weeks my sense of anticipation grew at the thought of a last day (or rather evening) in the life, but there was one slight concern – I had a ticket but Julia did not. I could look forward to sitting down to dinner at the Bradford Hilton, surrounded by some of the greats of the sport, but it would be without my beloved partner, the companion who had accompanied me from the start of this voyage of discovery. The physical distance between Rivington and Bradford is not great, but our emotional lives had changed so much (for the better) during the course of the journey between the two and I wished so much that the final steps would be made together. So, over a number days we hatched plan after plan to make the evening a shared experience, before going on to throw them all away on the grounds of impracticality. It was looking like I would be making my final trip (a short one along the M62) alone.

The day of the dinner arrived and still it seemed like there would be no place for Julia. However, had I checked my phone messages over the previous few days I would have known that a positive and generous outcome was in the offing. Looking out of the window early on Saturday 13th November, I saw that the skies were clear and cold and that a watery early winter sun was doing its best to bring some warmth to the day. These were ideal off-season riding conditions and I had arranged to go out during the day with Toni – a potter up and down the hills of the West Lancashire moors between Blackburn and Bolton. It was no coincidence that our route that day took in the climb of Winter Hill at Belmont and the descent into Rivington, scene of the National Championships and Commonwealth Games road race in 2002. As we travelled along the same road on which I had first seen Cheeky Phil I couldn't help but be aware of the milestones and symbols that surrounded me. The Barn café (a well-known meeting point for walkers and cyclists) and then the High School with its large playing field where spectators gathered to watch the races, were twin telling reminders of how the seeds of the story had been sewn.

The challenging terrain in the area ensured that we enjoyed a good workout and so we decided to stop for a well-earned lunch at a café on the outskirts of Horwich. As usual I had taken my mobile phone with me and as I prepared to tuck into a toasted bacon sandwich it rang. To my surprise the call was from Tom. Apparently Dudley had been trying to contact me for a few days to tell me that a last minute cry-off on the table booked by the British Cycling Federation meant that Julia now also had a seat for the dinner. Had I checked my voice mail messages I would already have known this. Tom told me Julia and I would be sitting at different but adjoining tables and this was good enough for me. I was also a little intrigued, as I had observed the relationship between the Fund and the BCF on a number of occasions during the year and noted that, nominally at least, they seemed to represent two different cultures as well as (sometimes competing) arms of the sport. I thanked Tom more than once before ringing home to tell Julia the news. I was so excited that the bacon sandwich was going cold before I stopped talking and took my first bite.

Full of coffee and warm from the rudimentary gas fire in the café and with an even greater sense of eagerness at the evening to come I rode the last miles home with a renewed sense of energy. The final few climbs seemed smaller and less steep than normal and we were home in what seemed like double quick time. After another coffee I said goodbye to Toni and we hurriedly began to prepare for the dinner.

Setting off in the late afternoon, we arrived in Bradford at around 6pm. The Hilton hotel we entered that night was markedly more busy and boisterous than the one I had walked into one Sunday morning around a year before. The lobby and bar area were full of people and it struck me then and there what a massive logistical exercise this must be for both the organisers of the event and for the hotel management. Later, I discovered that there were around 600 diners in attendance that night and this only increased my appreciation of their efforts. On first inspection, it appeared that none of the committee members of the Fund were around. At the same, time we were regularly witness to the familiar face of a current or past champion cyclist, as they moved past us. To onlookers such as us, however, they seemed less like themselves, dressed in suits and ties. Also, the fact that the dinner took place in November meant that many were a little fuller in the face than normal, adding to the slightly bizarre nature of the experience.

I went to the bar to order drinks. To my right stood a slim man in a shirt and tie. When he ordered, he spoke with the trace of a Liverpudlian accent and when I stole a quick glance across I saw that it was Chris Boardman; pursuit champion at the Barcelona Olympics, Tour de France prologue time-trial winner and world hour record holder (to name but a few of his many achievements in the sport). To those outside the sport he was probably that man on the funny black bike who wore the Darth Vader helmet, but here he was, just another member of the cycling fraternity doing his bit and having a good night out. This incident set the tone for the evening and it wasn't long before we caught a glimpse of Graham and Sam across the hotel lobby. They had arranged to stay in the hotel for the night and had made their way down from their room on one of the floors above. The lobby of a hotel felt like an apt place in which to catch up, as a number of our encounters, stretching as far back as our meeting in Beauvais early in the year, had taken place in such places. Shortly after, Tom emerged from a ante-room with some committee members and apparently they had all been in a briefing session, designed to ensure that the evenings events went well and to schedule. Although not formally involved in the organisation of the evening, Tom's family connections and long-standing friendship with men such as Dudley, meant that he had been drafted in to help. We managed brief conversations with both Graham and Tom before the diners were asked to take their seats and I couldn't resist the urge to ask them one more time if their plans for the 2005 season were any clearer. It was a hard habit to break, but neither had any concrete news, although it seemed that the night itself would provide opportunities to network with a range of people with team connections. If the right conversations took place, the dinner itself could have a bearing on their futures.

Having been asked to make our way to our tables, Julia and I had a slightly nervous time, knowing that we were going to be seated with groups that knew each other, but to whom we were strangers. I found myself seated next to Danny Horton, a respected ex-professional, whilst Julia was surrounded by the great and the good of British Cycling, including the President of the Federation, Brian Cookson. As this point the guest of honour, Eddy Merckx entered the room to loud applause, accompanied by Dudley and Hugh Porter, who was to act as MC for the evening. I was doing my best to settle in on the table, but Danny broke the ice by telling us of the time that he unintentionally stood on the foot of Merckx on the start line of the Barcelona World Championships in the 1970s. From then on, I felt at more at home. Having made sure that the great Merckx was settled on his table, Dudley then returned to his seat and heaved a sigh of relief. Apparently he had been in a room with Eddy before their presentation to the crowd and had found himself having to engage in small talk with someone that he obviously admired greatly and it seemed from his expression that he had been just a little overawed by the experience.

Dinner was then served and the talk and the drinks began to flow. I told my story for one of the last times, and they told me about their cycling careers and also of their own experiences of and relationships with Dave Rayner. It was an exhilarating and at some points a poignant time, and I noted once more how significant this young man had been in the lives of those whose paths he crossed. Also, at one point Danny talked about how injury had ended his own career and the remembrance of this difficult time, even down to how he had been forced to cut short what turned out to be his final serious training ride, left him in a slightly emotional state. This though soon passed and we moved onto the subject of golf, which was clearly now taking up much of his time and passion.

From time to time I glanced across to the next table and on each occasion I found Julia deep in conversation. It was nice to see that she too had settled in so well. Looking to other tables, again there was a sea of familiar faces. Table number one included Eddy Merckx (naturally), as well as Hugh Porter and Bradley Wiggins, the new Olympic pursuit champion and the man that I had mistakenly thought was a Credit Agricole team wannabe when I was taking part in a criterium race at Preston. Tom and Liv were on a table with Tom's family as well as Roger, whilst Graham and Sam were seated with Dan

Fleeman and some of the other young riders from the 2004 crop of the Fund. On another table I saw Malcolm Elliot, an ex-points jersey winner from the Tour of Spain, who, although now in his forties, had made a successful return to competition in the UK. On another sat Russell and Dean Downing who were among the best of current riders and who had been Graham's team-mates in 2003 at Life Repair. The list just seemed to go on and on. As dessert was being served, Chris Walker from the Committee of the Fund and himself a top racer in his day appeared at our table and began talking to Danny. Chris recounted a story of making an escape in a race with Danny in the very early part of his career. It was easy to sense the astonishment that Chris had clearly felt at being a young aspiring rider away up the road with someone as good and with as much standing as Danny and that sense of awe and wonder seemed to be in evidence for many people that night.

The end of dinner was the signal for Hugh Porter to conduct a series of interviews with some of the star guests of the evening, including Merckx himself as well as Bradley Wiggins and Roger. Looking dapper and slimmer than in previous years, Merckx was a fine interviewee, expressing himself impressed at the size of the turnout for the event. Sharing some memories from his experiences of riding with and against some of those present, he talked warmly of Tom Simpson and also about an occasion when he was outsprinted for second place in a race in the UK by Tom's Dad, Sid. Bradley Wiggins was clearly enjoying a purple period in his life. He jumped onto the stage sporting a broad smile to be interviewed by Hugh Porter. His happiness was not misplaced, as since his Olympic victory in August, he had been married and the newlyweds were now expecting their first child. It was not surprising that in the recent weeks he had, as he admitted, imbibed a wee bit too much alcohol than is altogether good for an elite athlete.

When Roger was interviewed, one of the main topics of discussion, alongside that famous April day of the Paris–Roubaix was how he would fare as a member of Lance Armstrong's Discovery Channel team. He told the crowd that he was due to travel to the US before Christmas to take part in a training camp and also in order to get to know his team-mates and there was much laughter at the fact that he had already been told by his new, ultra-professional employers that he would have to lose weight before the season began. Unsurprisingly, Roger came across as an intelligent, funny and humble man and there was no doubt in my mind that Tom must have learnt a great deal from him. More than this though, they were obviously now good friends.

Following the interviews there was a brief lull in the evening and I took the chance to switch tables to see how Julia's evening was unfolding. Surrounded by some of the most influential men in the sport, it was clear that she was enjoying her own place in the spotlight. It had transpired that Julia and Brian Cookson had a common link to Burnley (Julia having taught there and Brian coming from the area) and much of their conversation had been about the particular social and political issues that face this part of the world. Of course there was some talk of sport and Julia became aware of the historical reasons why the governing body and the Fund did not always seem to act in unison. However, as was typical of my own experiences, the differences were of approach rather than of aim. Both obviously wanted the best for the sport. Also, having returned from Athens with a clutch of medals that had made cycling one of the most successful sports for team Great Britain (at the same time ensuring that it retained a generous level of lottery funding) one couldn't really argue that the BCF's approach was not working.

During her conversations, Julia was also able to enjoy an insight from Brian into the psychological elements of the pressure cooker environment of the Olympic Games. As she was able to tell me later, some of the most assured and confident riders in the team were reduced to emotional wrecks by the pressure they felt to succeed, or perhaps more accurately, the pressure not to fail. Some were able to deal with this more assuredly than others, with a few being reduced to tears before they had even competed. Another interesting and funny aspect of spending time at Julia's table was in seeing one or two of the BCF party slightly the worse for wear. I too had a drink or two inside me (Julia drawing the short straw for driving duty that night) and probably wasn't as coherent as I would have chosen to have been, but I was perfectly fine and erudite in comparison with one or two of the other diners.

After some time with Julia I thought it right to have one final conversation with Graham and Tom, as well as some of the other people that I had met along the way. This was really an opportunity for me to say thank you. Thank you for allowing me into that world and for making me feel welcome. Thank you for putting up with me when I was asking questions on days when you would rather not talk. I made my way around the room with a pen and a copy of the programme of the evening's events and over the course of the next 30 minutes a rather drunken man could be seen perched by a series of tables gaining autographs and saying thanks – and at the same time his goodbyes. For many people these would not be the most sought-after signatures of the evening, but they were the ones that would mean the most to me. I returned to my seat with the programme and heaved a tired and emotional sigh of my own. Surrounding a black and white photograph of Dave Rayner astride a bike and in full racing kit were the names of Graham and Sam and Tom and Liv. In addition, before the evening ended I managed to catch up with Dudley and Keith once more and ensured that their autographs too found their way onto the front of the programme. The picture now sits in pride of place in my living room.

It was now time for the main fundraising element of the evening – an auction of a large number of pieces of cycling memorabilia. Supporters from all over the world had generously donated many items, including a US Postal jersey signed by their entire 2004 Tour de France team and the bids that they attracted did much to swell the coffers of the Fund. In total something in the region of £18,000 was raised on the night, as Hugh Porter and David Duffield managed to cajole and coerce the audience into higher and higher bids for the wide range of items on offer.

It was nearing midnight when the auction concluded, but

this was not the final entertainment of the evening. However as a DJ prepared to get the crowd on its feet, we decided that it was time to head back home. Returning to our car, we passed a content and slightly tipsy looking Bradley Wiggins and his expression as he hugged his partner and stroked the bump of her pregnancy seemed to sum up the whole evening for us. There was simply a lot of love in the room that night. It seemed that in no time Julia was pulling up the car outside our house at the conclusion of what had been a great way in which to bring our year to an end.

I awoke the following morning happy and feeling energetic. What better way to enjoy a quiet Sunday than by getting out on the bike. At around noon I rode over to Chorley where I knew there was a cyclo-cross event taking place in the main park. When I arrived, the scene that met me was in marked contrast to that of the previous night. Where the dinner had been full of glitz, today was about cold and mud and Wellington boots. The most interesting sight to strike me as I queued for a warm drink at a burger van was that of Hugh Porter. Again he was acting as the MC, but this time in a much more down-to-earth environment. However, I remember that he called out the largely unfamiliar names of the riders in the race with the all the enthusiasm that he had shown when introducing Eddy Merckx. It was good to see people giving something back to the sport and this was further reinforced by the sight of others that I had seen at the dinner now acting as race marshals.

In a short time I had travelled from the high table of cycling back to its grass roots and I had found both to be equally hospitable places. However, as I rode home in the gathering gloom of the afternoon I realised that this time it really was over. From now on I would be following Tom and Graham from a distance and just as a fan. I would be back on the other side of the ropes – getting my information second hand and looking on, rather than in some small way taking part.

Over the next few weeks I found myself scouring the internet and the cycling press for news whilst at the same time trying to resist the temptation to contact Graham and Tom directly. I was anxious to find out if they had they found a new ride for 2005 or if they were remaining with their current teams, but knew also that our relationship had to move on. If we were going to stay in touch it would be as friends, not as a writer and his subjects. In some ways we would have to start again and create a different kind of relationship. It was painfully obvious that I was missing them, their stories and the sense of adventure that merely being around them brought me. However, I couldn't kid myself and I knew deep down that I had truly reached the end of the last waltz.

CHAPTER 13

Good Souls

JANUARY 2005. The dust had settled and it was now time for me to try and make sense of all that had happened during the previous year. Although it had not been long, I could now attempt to put the series of fantastic adventures that I had been lucky enough to have experienced into some sort of perspective. There were the fundamental questions regarding the meaning of it all and the affects of the journey on all those that been involved, but at a more practical level I was also ready to contemplate the many and varied things that I had learned along the way. There was, for example, simply getting to know Tom and Graham. What had I had come to understand about them as bike riders and perhaps more importantly as people? What had I learned about the role and nature of the Dave Rayner Fund and the people who ran it? What, in turn, did this say about the wider cycling community in this country? And what about the sport itself? How (if at all) had cycling in Britain changed and developed during the course of the story? Finally, there were the many and varied people, places and experiences that I had come across. How had they affected me? There was certainly plenty to consider.

However, the first day of the year was marked by something altogether more homely and affectionate, but no less significant. It was a brief text message from Cheeky Phil wishing me a Happy New Year. I sent him one back, saying

'See you in August', when Julia and I would be back in Barneville-Carteret, once more enjoying its unpretentious charms and dreaming of quitting the rat race for a life by the sea. We had booked another summer holiday in our sleepy Normandy town and this time we had made sure that we would be there on the day of the Briquebec road race. I was determined that this year we would sit outside a bar on the main street to watch Phil (and maybe also Graham too) climb up the cobbled street past the shops and the castle before heading off for another lap of the local countryside.

Although only a small event, Phil's text message was a little reminder of the life-changing nature of the events of the previous year and again I had reason to say thanks to the curiosity that had driven me on to find out more about the life of the British bike rider in Europe. It meant that I now had memories I could cherish, safe in the knowledge that nothing could take them away and as the early days of the month passed I became aware that we were nearing the first anniversaries of a number of key events. There were, for example, my first meetings with Graham and Tom and Cheeky Phil and all the subsequent telephone calls and emails that followed and it dawned on me now that I couldn't help but see 2005 through the prism of 2004. As a result I often found myself looking back and attempting to put myself once more in the role of the newcomer. I was trying to re-create the feeling of meeting the young bike riders for the first time, of being slightly intimidated, but trying to appear calm. I was looking back at the person who had been sitting in the half-light with Phil at the Manchester Velodrome telling him just how close we had come to meeting on more than one occasion. It was, however, hard to return to this particular place. In fact, in some ways it was like looking at someone else and I began to realise that the very process of chasing a dream changes a person. In addition, and at a more basic level, I was aware of the fact that I now simply knew a lot more about cycling, with all its subtleties and nuances, than I had done previously.

But what of Graham and Tom? What is there to say about

the two guys that made the whole thing possible? My first response is that both were generous and giving to even let me follow them in the first place. Also, neither sought to hide away even when they were tired or injured or just plain pissed off and both were willing to let me into their lives in a way that many people just wouldn't. Without this openness there would have been little for me to write about. Of course they were a little wary, especially in the early stages. Conversations could at times be a little stilted, but this was understandable and as time passed our meetings became less and less formal, to the extent that it became just two people catching up for a coffee and a chat. I was glad to be able to relegate the tape recorder I had bought for the project to a drawer, safe in the knowledge that it was no longer necessary. It was also rewarding to find both Graham and Tom interested in my own (limited) progress as a bike rider and similarly, they both seemed to hit it off right away with Julia which made for even more of a shared experience. Very simply, in their different ways they went well beyond the call of duty and imposed no real restrictions on our working relationship.

One of my few regrets (perhaps not theirs) is that I didn't get to spend more time with them during the course of the year. Often our meetings were all too brief and the time pressures that we all faced meant that I often had to cut to the chase of news gathering. As if to exemplify the point, I recall the times fondly when we were able to just chat as some of the most informative and rewarding parts of the whole thing: over dinner with Graham and Sam in Aylesbury, or in Roger's living room with Tom and Liv. It was on these occasions that I learnt the most about them as people: what they liked and disliked; how they coped with their often chaotic lifestyles; who they looked up to; how they made ends meet. And what I found was that here were a couple of ordinary people, but both of them doing extraordinary things. Ask Graham or Tom about what they did at the weekend and you would hear a wealth of stories and ones that many people (if they understood their significance) would envy greatly. I represented my country, or I won a big race in France, or I went out training with the

British champion or I spent all day in a group with Basso and Zabel. The list just goes on and on and these were just some of addictive experiences, the stellar memories, that both Graham and Tom had at the end of their year.

I also learned that they were very different bike riders too. Or rather that they were at different points in their development. Tom was riding at a higher level than Graham and although a consistently solid performer, he had in some ways become accustomed to a place in the middle of the peloton. It is incredibly hard to be a winner in Belgium and Tom had gone close on a number of occasions. However, I sensed that he struggled to maintain that tiny element of self-belief that allows you to think: Today I'm going to win. This was not a criticism of him, as it seemed that many a young bike rider went through this wearing down process when moving into the big pond of the professional ranks. At the same time, Tom was lucky enough to have an advantage over others in that his Dad had ridden at a high level himself and so understood the pressures. Also, living in the same environment as Roger would be a great counter-balance to any feelings of self-doubt. In the case of Roger, this was not just because he himself was successful, but also because we was self-effacing, generous and supportive, in an older brother kind of way, to both Tom and Matt.

Tom was also an ultra pragmatist in his attitude to two-wheeled battle and the intense demands of the life. It seemed that he had learned over time to adapt to the requirements of the day- in, day-out nature of the competition and could switch in and out of race mode very easily and quickly. At one level this should not be surprising. Cycling was his job and a professional approach was necessary in order to impress team-mates and opponents alike. However, he was honest enough to admit that it had not always been this way.

What impressed me the most though, was Tom's ability to be calm and (to use the dreaded sporting cliché) focused, whilst at the same time never losing sight of how fortunate he was to be in Belgium riding his bike for a living. The element of romance never left him although he knew that there were easier ways to make a buck and that many of his friends from university were well on the way to having the material rewards that he lacked. Although you can't place a fulfilled dream on the sideboard for visitors to admire, it is no less important. In fact, I had come to realise through meeting Graham and Tom that dreams and aspirations are in fact much more significant than possessions. However, at the same time Tom also knew that there would be plenty of time in the future, when this particular adventure had run its course, for Sunday visits to Ikea. In the intervening period, though, he would continue to live his dream for all it was worth.

For Graham 2004 was a tough year, but one in which he had learnt a great deal. He had been forced to face up to a series of challenges from the moment he found out that he was not going to be a full-time member of the Great Britain under-23 squad. This would have been his preferred career option, and it took him quite a while to overcome the disappointment of being omitted from the final selection. However, he didn't dwell on his misfortune for too long and instead put himself back in the shop window, in time to secure the support of the Fund and a place with a French team.

Looking back, it is clear that moving to Beauvais was always going to be a test and Graham's early victory in Paris–Evreux perhaps only served to postpone the onset of the hard reality of being away from home in an alien environment, with a group of strangers. Also, it is hard to underestimate how difficult it was for Graham and Sam to be apart for long periods over the summer. The loneliness and the boredom would at some points have been difficult for both to bear, but at least Sam had the support systems of family and friends around her. It is to the great credit of this young couple that they stayed the course and in some ways seemed closer than ever at the end of the year. It seemed to the onlooker that Graham spent 2004 learning many of the hard and universal lessons that are dished out to the young talented sportsman. By definition Tom must have also faced the same ones when he first moved abroad and in one sense you could see Graham as the before picture and Tom as the after. However, it was important for me never to lose sight of them as individuals.

A key factor in one's attempts to become a top-level sportsman seems to be how you deal with becoming a commodity. Other people start to define you, not by who you are, but by what you did on the bike today. In some ways, a young rider has to adjust to being treated as a piece of meat. At the same time you must learn to not take it personally and to accept good days and bad days with almost equal indifference. To most team managers, fans and journalists you are just another man on a bike. Your talent is a given (you wouldn't even be here otherwise) and they don't really care why you're not winning or why you have 'packed' during a race. All that counts to them is whether you are a winner or a loser. This is the hard and unforgiving side of the life and it is not for everyone. However, for many it is the accepted trade-off for doing what you love for a living and of one day being that winner. This I feel was something that Graham encountered for the first time in 2004 and he sometimes found it a difficult transition to make, but by the end of the season he certainly knew the score.

The support Graham received from the Dave Rayner Fund must have helped enormously in this regard. The Fund is obviously very interested in the results of its young charges and needs to produce successful riders in order to maintain its profile and the support of the cycling public. However, its role is much wider than this. As I had seen early on through the experiences of Cheeky Phil, the Fund offer opportunities for the recipients of its support to blossom as people as well as cyclists. Every year a group of young men and women live their own dreams and it is not unusual for these to develop beyond what was initially envisaged. In short, the Fund helps people to broaden their horizons and to re-think what is possible. I thought of this when Graham and Sam told me of how they had spent Bastille Day, in an idyllic beauty spot surrounded by local people enjoying their national holiday. Whatever else had happened, here was the kind of unusual experience that a young couple from Doncaster would now have with them forever.

I can't say enough good things about the men behind the Fund. Very simply they took a real tragedy and somehow managed to turn it into something positive and rewarding. No mean feat, especially when it was done in the midst of their own grief. Now, over ten years on, they have an organisation that is stronger and more influential than ever and they can afford to be proud of what they have achieved. The guys, however, are not prone to such outbursts of emotion. They are very much products of their own experiences and are understated men of true substance. As with so many other people that crossed my path, I feel privileged to have come to know some of them fairly well.

An almost omniscient presence throughout the journey was Dave Rayner himself. I did not know Dave, but felt his influence over the story from the first day I met Dudley, Keith and Bill Holmes. In the time that followed I was forced on more than one occasion to prove that my intentions were positive and would in no way tarnish the memory of their friend. However, I accepted this as part of the deal and knew that ultimately it was a simple reflection of the love and the loss that was still felt by those that had known him. It's no accident that it is Dave's picture that now sits in my living room and it acts as a reminder to me of the supreme sacrifice that lies at the heart of the story. He must have been very special.

But what of the wider sport? One of the things that struck me during the course of the year was the sense that cycling in the UK was entering a purple period. It seemed to me, to be developing into a well-run, high-profile sport that contrary to the common lazy perception of being the last home of the unchallenged drug cheat, actually had worthy values and ethics, and with them a growing level of credibility. Brian Cookson (the President of the BCF) had impressed me when we met briefly at the dinner and I thought that with people like this at the helm, we could be happy that things would continue to develop in the right direction. More than anything else, Brian and his colleagues struck me as genuine in their ambition to make British cycling a home for clean winners. I knew that there would always be conflict between the old school and the new approach and recognise that it is just hard for some people to get used to change. This though is one of life's eternal truths and when I compared the scene at Rivington in 2002 to that at the Celtic Manor in 2004, I was in no doubt that things were moving forwards.

And then there was my own year. I would be lying if I said that it was a hardship to spend a summer working my way around the UK and Europe in search of men on bikes. Sometimes it put a large dent in my bank balance, but it was great, great fun. I think that for some people in fact, it was too much of a good thing. The looks I received when I told people of the latest excursion – Paris, Dublin, Brussels and so on, and the adventures that unfolded at every step, were often a mixture of disbelief and incredulity. It was as if in some small way I should be apologising for chasing my own dream whilst documenting those of Graham and Tom. However, it was at these points that I switched sports to rugby league (my other great sporting passion) to remind myself of the Wayne Bennett book. Wayne Bennett is the coach of the Brisbane Broncos (perhaps the most successful club team of the modern era) and he has a regular newspaper column. A selection of his thought-provoking and positivist pieces was brought together a few years back and the ensuing book was entitled 'Don't Die with the Music in You'. As I recovered from illness it became my mantra and unknowingly I think that it must be that of Graham and Tom, of Cheeky Phil, of Brain Cookson and the BCF and of Dudley and the Dave Rayner Fund.

Cynics could say that I didn't do enough to explore the more morally ambiguous elements of top-level sport and I suppose I won't ever know what people chose not to tell me. However, my very early conscious decision was that the world simply did not need one more exposé on the dodgy world of cycling. Look in the sports section of any bookshop and you will already see many examples of the sporting exposé. Also, to adopt such an approach would have been to abuse the trust and faith that everyone had shown in me. I didn't though find my chosen line of attack confining. Actually it was the opposite. Without an agenda to either whitewash or to dig dirt,

I felt free to be honest and open in the way I dealt with the negative stories that were going on in the background.

In addition to my links with the principal characters there were also many other newfound friendships and acquaintances to look back on and associations with places that otherwise would not feature in my own story. They continue to stay with me as events fade into memory. I can't predict where and when they will next crop up. Sometimes the milestones are huge and public, but at other moments, such as when my phone beeped and the name 'Cheeky' appeared on the display unit of the handset, they are much more intimate. They run through the whole range of emotions from the tragic, through the poignant, onto the entertaining and comic, before coming to a halt somewhere around the frankly bizarre. They are in sights and sounds and in tastes. Duvell beer in Belgium with Tom, Jez and Hilton, or homemade cakes in the village hall at the under-23 road race at Oakley. Hamish Haynes and his awful-looking cauliflower cheese in the student dorms of Newport (how does he race with one of those inside him?). They are in the weather too. A particular kind of unceasing torrent is Friday the 13th in Leuven and a sunny spring day is forever Hillingdon, waiting for Tom while the race officials mop the blood off the tarmac and the ambulances cart the injured off to hospital. It's even in transport. Bikes obviously. Both Graham and Tom rode Ridleys (a Belgium manufacturer) and they are frequent sites on the pages of cycling magazines. However, it is also hard to pass a mobile home without for a small moment wondering if it belongs to the Barras family. The symbols are big and they are small, but what is true is that they will always be there, lurking around the corner. They'll be in the shadows waiting to bring me up short at the thought of a race, of a smile or of a tear. They are seemingly small interruptions, side shows to the main events of the day, but they now have a power to bring something of 2004 back into the clearest of views.

One night early in the month I was watching the Tour Down Under (the early season Australian stage race) on TV and there was a small crash in the field during the opening city-centre criterium. A member of the Navigators team had come down and on closer inspection the commentator Phil Liggett (who it seems must now have finally surfaced after the end of last year's Rayner's ride) announced that the grumpy-looking bloke who was brushing himself down was one Hilton Clarke. I wouldn't claim to have any deep relationship with Hilton, but I did share with him the experience of doing around 60mph whilst he was holding onto the team car, and all the time with an improperly fitted back wheel all set to fall out. Of course, we were on opposite sides of the passenger door, but for all that there were only centimetres between us and I can still recall as if it was yesterday the yell of fear he gave when he realised that his wheel was loose.

Similarly when I picked up Cycling Weekly to see a picture of Roger Hammond in his new Discovery Channel kit, out on a training ride in Texas with Lance Armstrong, I could smile a slightly more knowing smile and imagine the shirt drying out on the back of a radiator in Roger's living room. Visiting the Velodrome always brings back memories of Phil and when we went there to watch one of the Revolution track meetings it had the same effect. As Julia and I watched Ed Clancy and Mark Cavendish from the Great Britain under-23 team tearing up the track our thoughts went back to the day at Oakley when 'Cav' consoled Graham and tried to fix him up with some medical help from the BCF, before confessing to how much weight he had put on during a period off the bike with a virus. The point I am trying to make here is that in the past I would have appreciated them all as tremendous bike riders, but would have known nothing of them as individuals. I would not have had an insight into their personalities, their senses of humour, their failings – their humanity. It all just seemed more real now.

It started off as a story about cycling, but in the end it finished up as a story of love. Everyone that took the trip seemed in one way or another to have been motivated by the most powerful of positive feelings and the overall effect was to act as an antidote to the cynical world in which we all live. For the cyclists there was the love of being a winner, the love of living the life and the love of just riding the bike. However, at the same time there was the love of people for people. There were the many, like Tom, who loved and still miss Dave Rayner, but who had fashioned something noble and worthy from his untimely death. There was Graham and his love for Sam and there was Cheeky Phil and his new unimagined life in France. In the background I felt a renewed love for Julia. The whole thing was a simply a blast from start to finish and now that it is over I need to steal once more from Wayne Bennett to remind you for one last time 'Don't Die with the Music in You'.